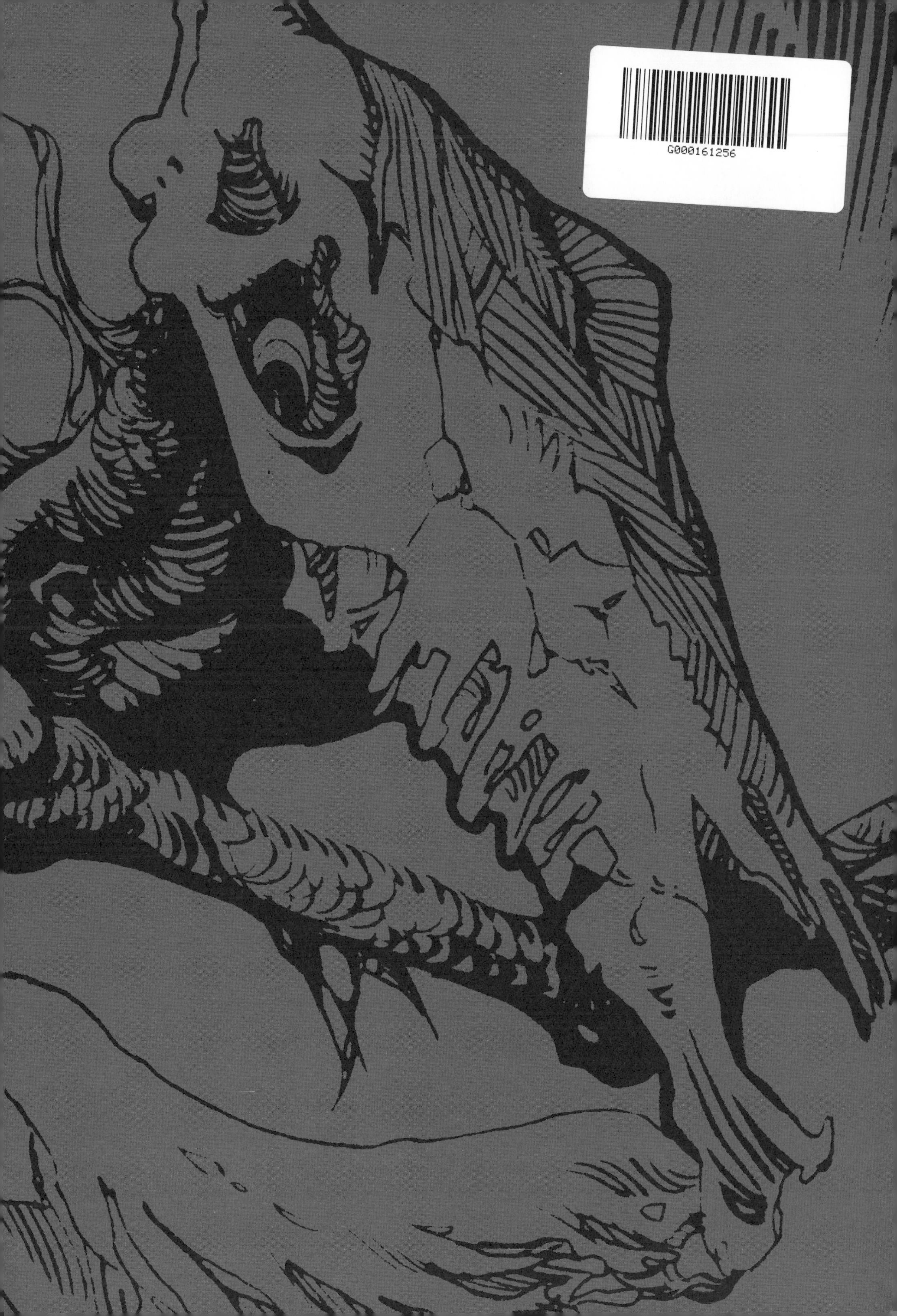

Esteban Maroto

LOVECRAFT
THE MYTH OF CTHULHU

IDW

Become our fan on Facebook **facebook.com/idwpublishing**
Follow us on Twitter **@idwpublishing**
Subscribe to us on YouTube **youtube.com/idwpublishing**
See what's new on Tumblr **tumblr.idwpublishing.com**
Check us out on Instagram **instagram.com/idwpublishing**

ISBN: 978-1-68405-125-0   21 20 19 18 1 2 3 4

COVER BY
ESTEBAN MAROTO

COVER COLOR BY
SANTI CASAS

TRANSLATION BY
ANNA ROSENWONG

EDITED BY
JUSTIN EISINGER
AND ALONZO SIMON

PRODUCTION BY
RON ESTEVEZ

PUBLISHER
TED ADAMS

Ted Adams, CEO & Publisher
Greg Goldstein, President & COO
Robbie Robbins, EVP/Sr. Graphic Artist
Chris Ryall, Chief Creative Officer
David Hedgecock, Editor-in-Chief
Laurie Windrow, Senior VP of Sales & Marketing
Matthew Ruzicka, CPA, Chief Financial Officer
Lorelei Bunjes, VP of Digital Services
Jerry Bennington, VP of New Product Development

Esteban Maroto

LOVECRAFT
THE MYTH OF CTHULHU

Introduction to the Cthulhu Mythos

"H.P. Lovecraft has yet to be surpassed as the twentieth century's greatest practitioner of the classic horror tale."

STEPHEN KING

I

You have just unlocked a lost and forgotten treasure chest, a Pandora's Box that will open a portal between our world and that of horror from beyond time and space. In a perfect fusion of content and form, the prodigious Esteban Maroto illustrates three classic short stories by the creator of cosmic horror, H. P. Lovecraft. These comic adaptations had been missing for far too many years. They are finally being presented here in a complete and definitive edition.

Maroto exhibits here a facet of his work for which he is often less recognized: master of terror. As a matter of fact most readers don't realize that with over a hundred comic stories he was the second most prolific contributor to Warren Publishing's line of horror anthologies: **Creepy**, **Eerie**, and **Vampirella**. Instead Maroto is best known in the U.S. for his fantasy art in the limited series **Atlantis Chronicles** (DC Comics, 1991) and his unforgettable recreation of the character Red Sonja, which due to a change of clothes, turned her into an internationally famous erotic icon.

There are clear reasons why the editors of horror comics found in Maroto the perfect artist. He draws the human figure with great dexterity, elegance, and sensuality. He has created images of fantasy women in particular that marked an era in comics and have been often imitated but never surpassed. His storytelling is impeccably clear and smooth. His comics can be understood even without reading the text, which, as we shall see later, is not that common. Finally, Maroto invented a kind of "accumulations of decorative information," so to speak, combining elements of Art Nouveau, the drawing style of illustrators like Arthur Rackham and Edmund Dulac, and design elements of psychedelic posters from the sixties and seventies. The artist distilled these influences and incorporated them into personal and unique results. These motifs enrich most of his stories, and become central elements in these adaptations, where complex nightmare images have to be visualized. Few artists could combine the realism and beauty of the first pages of each story with wild hallucinations that are revealed later. In fact, fellow artist Josep María Beà had said that "Lovecraft cannot be interpreted graphically, he is an example of literary subjectivism…, The mind of readers will generate its own monster in relation to psychic content reshuffled from their own culture and experiences. The interpretation of Lovecraftian universe is not transferable." In this book Maroto proves just the opposite. Although it is true that each reader generates their personal versions of these creatures, the same can be said of all the visual adaptations of any literary work. It is just a matter of degree, and although Lovecraft's supernatural beings are more apt to an individual elucidation than others, the writer detailed, sometimes minutely, the appearance of many of his fantastical beings. In fact, he even made a fairly precise drawing of his most famous one: Cthulhu.

II

The two key writers of short stories in the history of the horror genre are Edgar Allan Poe (1809-1849) and H.P. Lovecraft (1890-1937). Their influence extends far beyond literature and has affected many authors, artists, and filmmakers, inspiring them to create works based on their tales. Poe has been translated to other mediums much more frequently than Lovecraft. The visual richness of his stories makes them very suitable subjects for adaptations. Lovecraft on the other hand, wrote mostly about immense cosmic creatures. This explains the relative scarcity of comic adaptations of his stories, even though nearly one hundred years after their publication, they are now more popular than ever.

Since its inception in the form of comic strips in the late nineteenth century, comics have been a medium where creators were able to unleash their wildest fantasies. But the horror genre in particular did not appear in comics until the forties, when comics left newspapers and began to be sold as staple-bound pamphlets, the so-called comic books. That is when they stopped being solely geared to whole families (particularly children) and could venture into far darker themes.

One publisher in particular, the infamous EC Comics, specialized in terror. For the first time in 1951 they published three adaptations of Lovecraft. They were done by the great team of Al Feldstein (writer), Graham Ingels, and Jack Kamen (artists) in their anthologies **Weird Science** and **The Vault of Horror**. But just three years later, EC stopped publishing due to a witch hunt against comics in the United States Congress. It resulted in the creation of an industry organization for internal censorship (The Comics Code Authority) that prohibited explicitly the publication of comics with themes of the occult, supernatural, or explicit violence.

It took two decades for censorship to somewhat relax, and by the beginning of the seventies there was a new wave of "scary" comics being published that included more adaptations of Lovecraft. Author and editor Roy Thomas, a great admirer of pulp writers, promoted and adapted these stories. They were published in several Marvel Comics publications (**Tower of Shadows**, **Journey Into Mystery**), and illustrated by some of the best artists working for them at the time, like Barry Windsor-Smith, Johnny Craig, Tom Palmer, and Gene Colan.

Meanwhile two events had happened in the North American publishing industry that allowed the world of comics to circumvent the censorship. One was the emergence of underground comics, which ignoring the Comics Code, were aimed at adults and allowed to explicitly address all kinds of taboos. Influenced by EC Comics, far bloodier adaptations of Lovecraft's stories appeared in them. These included a masterful adaptation of "The Rats in the Walls" by genius Richard Corben (**Skull Comics** #5).

Also faithfully following the formula of EC Comics, James Warren created several anthologies of comics in black and white, not as comic books for children. This allowed him to avoid censorship. But despite adapting Poe more than twenty times, Lovecraft was only adapted twice. Fortunately one of these was a magnificent version of "Cold Air"(**Eerie** #82) by Bernie Wrightson, the artistic heir to Graham Ingels.

But in any of these adaptations no one dared to touch stories belonging to the so-called Cthulhu Mythos, for which Lovecraft is best known. In those thirteen canonical stories, the author created a world populated by immense and millenary cosmic entities,

which have been on Earth since the beginning of time, lurking just beyond the visible universe. Finally in 1972 the Uruguayan/Argentinean master Alberto Breccia decided to interpret these insane stories with the help of writer Norberto Buscaglia. The result is a set of essential works, not only for fans of Lovecraft, but also for any serious lover of the comics medium. In them Breccia fluctuated between a fine realism, expressionism, and almost complete abstraction, using pictorial and iconographic methods unknown in comics up to that point. Buscaglia, however, not only did not innovate in the textual part, but quite the opposite: he wrote huge explanatory captions for each panel, making these resemble illustrated stories, rather than comics.

III

This volume includes adaptations of the first three stories Lovecraft wrote that belong to the cycle called the Cthulhu Mythos. Lovecraft did not invent this name, other writers of his circle did. All have in common the presence of mysterious cults that summon evil creatures of cosmic origin and great powers, often in remote places of the earth.

"The Nameless City" is the first story Lovecraft wrote which relates directly to the Cthulhu mythology. It contains the first mention of the legendary book, the Necronomicon, which links these stories in their knowledge of ancient races. As is usual, the narrator writes in first person. Lovecraft said the story was inspired by one of his dreams, and the explicitly dreamlike quality of his discovery is evident.

"The Festival" happens in the imaginary city of Kingsport, and like the others, is part of the group of stories called the Arkham Cycle, which take place in New England. It is a sacrilegious Christmas story, which takes place below the basement of a church, where a procession of silent inhuman-looking hooded figures descend to the depths of the earth. This time, Maroto added a sacrifice not described in the original story.

"The Call of Cthulhu" is in the opinion of many experts the first great work by Lovecraft. The author himself was not convinced but his friend Robert E. Howard said it was "a masterpiece, which I am sure will live as one of the highest achievements of literature. Mr. Lovecraft holds a unique position in the literary world; he has grasped, to all intents, the worlds outside our paltry ken." It is considered the first mature work by the author and it combines stories within stories masterfully. For the first time Lovecraft consolidates his cosmology and portrays terror that spreads beyond the Earth into the stars. The comics adaptation of this story, by Buscaglia and Breccia, summarized much of the plot and broke its perfect triptych structure. Despite its great graphic merit, Breccia did not illustrate many important scenes, which were only mentioned in captions. And in the last pages of this previous adaptation, the images become incomprehensible, and they are totally reliant on the text. Because of this, Maroto's version, at thirty-two pages long, is the definitive one.

IV

The publication history of these comics is somewhat complex. The Spanish publisher Editorial Brugera commissioned them in the early eighties for a series of graphic novels that were to be collected in paperback format, adapting to comics authors like Isaac Asimov and Chester Himes, by artists such as Fernando Fernandez, Luis Bermejo, and Florenci Clavé. Maroto's three stories would have appeared in one of these volumes, followed by other volumes of Lovecraft tales adapted by Alex Niño and Sergio Toppi. But Brugera went out of business before Maroto finished his part and the collection was canceled. Three years later they were finally published in the back pages of the children's comics anthology *Capitán Trueno*. They never returned the originals to the artist, which is an unfortunately too common story in this field. These were mostly unseen, until Richard Ashford decided to publish them in the United States. Cross Plains released a version, translated into English by Maroto's friend Roy Thomas. Unfortunately, the cover was commissioned to Frank Brunner instead of Maroto, and its limited distribution made this edition virtually unnoticed.

V

Today Lovecraft continues to inspire many comics. You can see his influence on creators like Richard Corben and Jan Strand (*Ragemoor*), Grant Morrison and Chris Burnham (*Nameless*), Mike Mignola (*Hellboy*), Scott Snyder and Sean Murphy (*The Wake*), Ed Brubaker and Sean Phillips (*Fatale*), Steve Niles and Ben Templesmith (*Criminal Macabre*), Joe Hill

and Gabriel Rodriguez (*Locke and Key*)... Even the great Alan Moore has spent the last few years writing multiple stories inspired by the author, including his comics masterpiece *Providence*.

But there are not many faithful adaptations of his stories. Those that have been published in the last thirty years are, almost entirely, made by small publishers taking advantage that the original stories' status are in the public domain. They have often been adapted by amateurs, novices and enthusiasts, and not by great comics creators. Lovecraft remains largely unknown for the general public: admired and recognized, but seldom read. The image of Cthulhu decorates all kinds of products and merchandise. But his books, sometimes hard to read since they can be so dense, have yet to be adapted to the big or small screen with any success. They are influential and ignored simultaneously. This is in part why the reappearance of these adaptations is an important event. They are both a faithful interpretation of the originals and fully consistent with the rest of Esteban Maroto's oeuvre.

So now, dear reader, open this buried treasure to examine its contents carefully, and while you do, try to keep most of the lights in your house on. Otherwise, don't be surprised if you suddenly feel an unexplained cool breeze, and, perhaps suddenly, the faint touch of something moist and elusive.

Then you will know that ... Cthulhu lives!

José Villarrubia
Baltimore, March 2016
Adapted for this edition in November 2017

Prologue

"H. P. Lovecraft is the twentieth century horror story's dark and baroque prince."

STEPHEN KING

To read Lovecraft and to dwell on his stories produces a strange sensation of anxiety and terror. And yet this author and his myths wield a morbid, fatal attraction.

His stories warn us of the dangers that exist when someone investigates or gets too close to the unknown, attracting attention from malignant forces and being annihilated by the strange beings in our own mind.

Because myths are entities too powerful to be overcome by humans, he warns us that there are "shadowy forces that could destroy us if they so much as grunted in their sleep" (Stephen King, **Danse Macabre**). It is all too easy to lose control when we encounter living manifestations of the incomprehensible, situations where the risk of madness is tangible and terrifying.

Lovecraft felt like an alien in his own country and world; he said that humanity is but a small and insignificant blip in the cosmos, and the product of a spirit that seems to be everywhere except in human beings. He said that science might seem powerful and boundless, but was leading us toward a bleak future, toward chaos and a new Dark Age. A century later, such a thought has no place in our technological, materialistic universe.

I am dismayed by Lovecraft's racist theories, and by his lifelong depression. He lived a short, solitary life littered with letters, more than a hundred thousand, which is remarkable for someone who died at just 47 (1890-1937). He felt rejected and threatened by the society in which he lived. He was always—or always felt—terribly ill (he said he couldn't abide temperatures below 68 degrees) and, in spite of all his eccentricities, won devotees and followers across America, who not only disseminated his influence around the world, but since his death have made him one of the most honored masters of the genre.

The primary themes of his stories were always:

- forbidden knowledge
- otherworldly influences on humanity
- ancestral and atavistic guilt
- the impossibility of escaping destiny
- threats to civilization
- racism and other types of discrimination such as his well-established misogyny (in fact, women rarely appear in his work)

Without a doubt, fear of the unknown is intrinsic to humanity. But at the same time, the struggle to *understand* is equally a part of us. We carry rebellion in our genes, but—at least as far as I'm concerned—this is not a sin. Rather, it is liberation.

If gods do exist, then we are a part of them. And if they disappear, so too dies—or is transformed—a minute part of us. It may perhaps sound stupid or vain, but I did not ask for life, just as I would not ask for death. Perhaps it'd be best to quote Omar Khayyám (the ninth-century Persian poet):

"If those who have not yet come into the world knew the miseries which await them, truly they would never come.

"Life was given me without asking, and I think of returning it with scorn."

In a small corner of the universe,
2016 years after a fanciful,
but agreed-upon, century zero.

Esteban Maroto

Preface

In 1982, Editorial Bruguera began **Firmado por...**, a series of comic adaptations of classic genre stories (adventure, horror, science fiction) by writers like Isaac Asimov, Chester Himes, and Emilio Salgari, to name a few. They asked me to take on the three first pieces encompassed in the Cthulhu Mythos, and I was thrilled to accept, as I've always been fascinated by H. P. Lovecraft.

In order to strengthen the coherence between these three works, the publishers asked that I make the various "monsters" visually similar, and suggested that they look something like the creatures that my friend Alex Niño created for his book **Satan's Tears**. Since that time, I've cherished my friendship with him, and I treasure my copy of the book and the original drawings that he gave me (which were fortunately saved from the recent fire in my home and studio).

Unfortunately, Bruguera declared bankruptcy shortly before the first volume was set to appear. I don't think Alex got to draw even one page of the second. The commission never came.

It was quite an ordeal to get ahold of my work again, but I finally managed. However, I was never able to recover the originals, lost like so many others in those times when such things were far more complicated than they are today.

Oddly, Ediciones B, which inherited the project, ended up publishing fragments of my work in the magazine **Capitán Trueno**. And later, I got word of a strange American edition with my pictures but new text by Roy Thomas, which Cross Plains published quietly in 2000, and with which I am in no way satisfied.

With the originals lost, some old copies I had in my personal archive came to light in the fire (an interesting paradox, isn't it?), which is when I decided to publish them independently. But in this, I was unsuccessful. Now, David Hernándo and Editorial Planeta have arrived to bring this old project to a happy conclusion at long last.

In hindsight—34 years having now passed—I wouldn't illustrate these myths the same way. I believe that today's new technology offers excellent tools to represent and better disseminate extremely complex stories; but at the same time, I ask myself if this might not sacrifice spontaneity and fall into the very trap Lovecraft warned us about: "the widespread growth of cultural misinterpretation." And let us not forget the essential component of art: magic.

How is it possible for the two dimensions of paper to represent a universe of sensations, shapes, and strange feelings, in unknown realities and dimensions? Unlike the stories' creator, I have faith in humanity. Despite all our flaws and shortcomings, we strive ever onward, not toward a new Dark Age, but into an age of understanding and light. I once read somewhere that we cannot choose our destiny, but we can choose the path we take toward it.

Moreover, I believe that this path, this quest, does not lead to an endpoint or a final solution. The world is changing at an incredible speed, like a possessed geometric progression, which scarcely gives us time today to process the consequences of yesterday's actions.

What is truly important is to awaken interest in the things around us and inside us, whether spiritual, material, or imaginary. For me, there is nothing worse than apathy, ignorance, and submission to the status quo.

In this quest, I have always found fellow travelers, and I am sure there are many among you. Thank you... and let us continue living while fate allows.

**In the same corner,
with the same ship of dreams.**

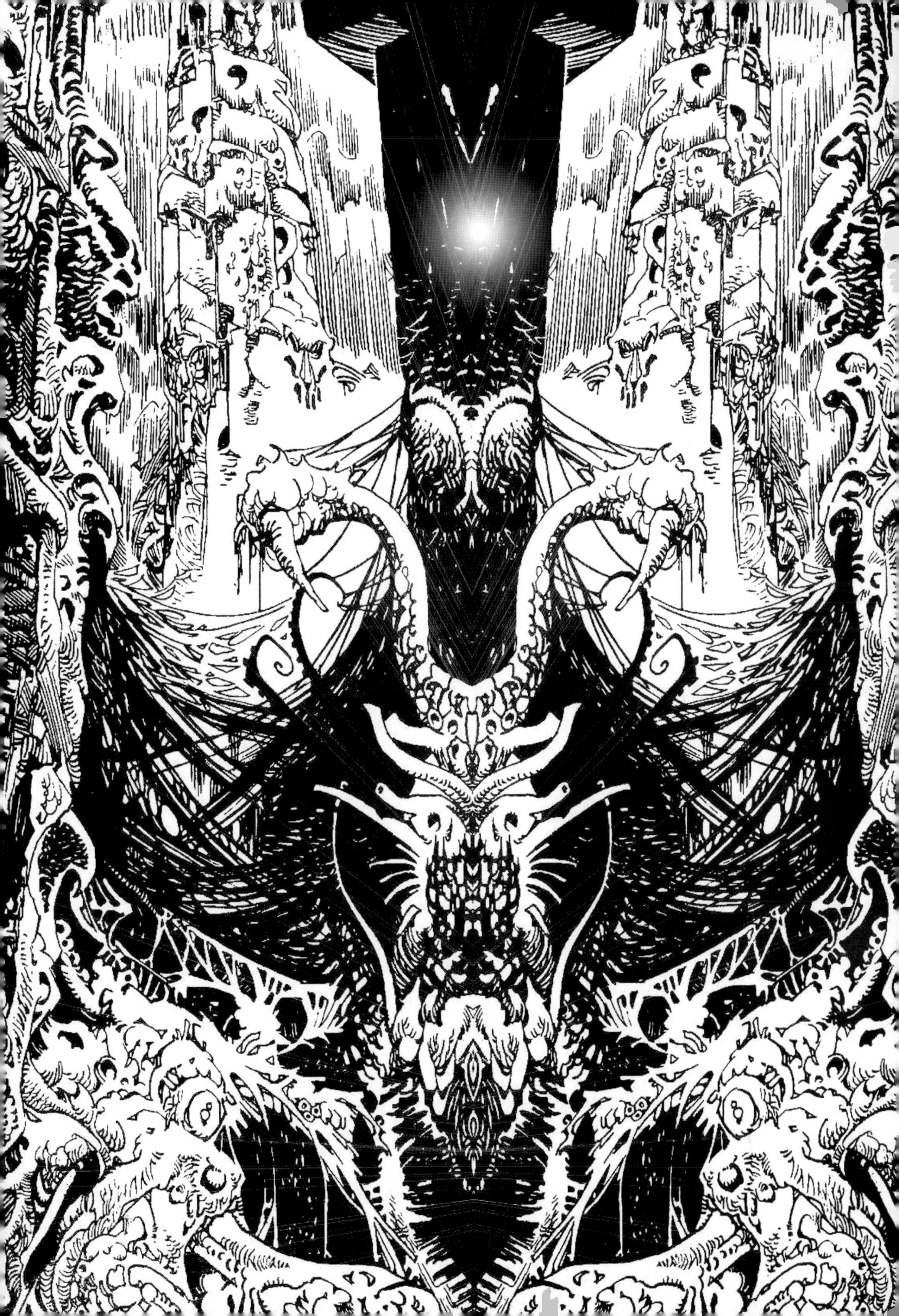

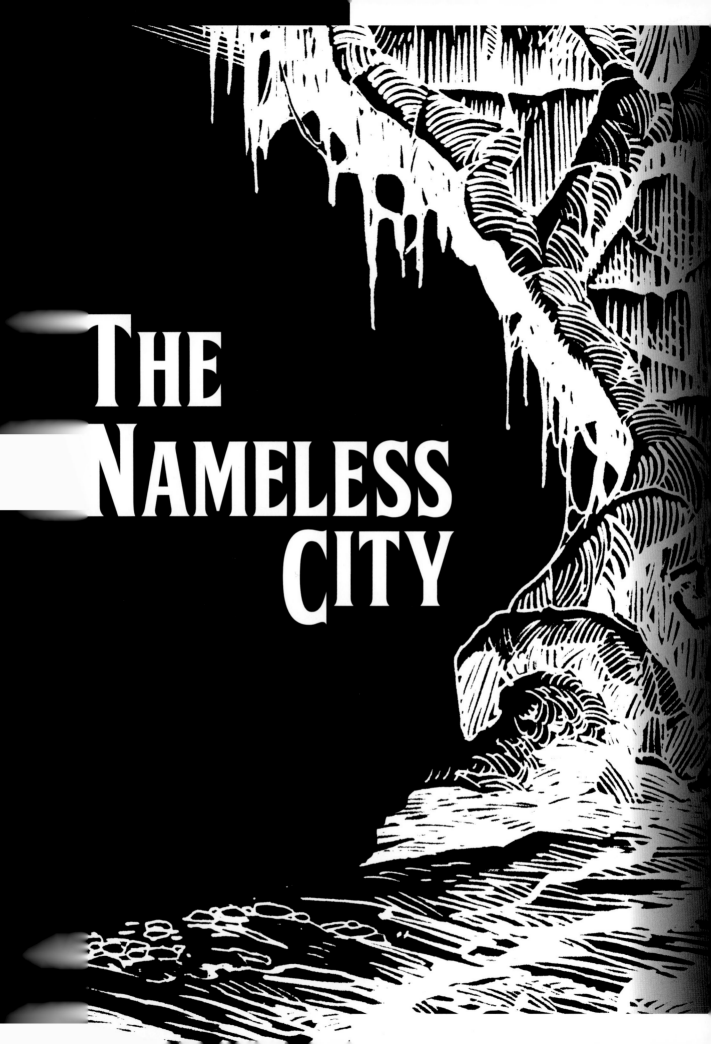

THE
NAMELESS
CITY

...THAT IS NOT DEAD WHICH CAN ETERNAL LIE...

...AND WITH STRANGE AEONS EVEN DEATH MAY DIE.

REMOTE IN THE
DESERT OF ARABY LIES
THE NAMELESS CITY.

NO ONE RECALLS IF IT WAS EVER ALIVE, NOR WHO
BUILT IT. THERE IS NO LEGEND SO OLD AS TO GIVE
IT A NAME, BUT IT IS TOLD OF IN WHISPERS AROUND
CAMPFIRES AND MUTTERED ABOUT BY GRANDAMS IN
THE TENTS OF SHEIKS, SO THAT ALL THE TRIBES
SHUN IT WITHOUT WHOLLY KNOWING WHY.

ONE NIGHT, ABDUL ALHAZRED, THE MAD POET
DREAMED OF THE PLACE WHERE THE NAMELESS
CITY COULD BE FOUND.

THE NEXT DAY, HE WROTE IN HIS GHASTLY
JOURNAL INEXPLICABLE POEMS AND A BRIEF
DESCRIPTION OF THE NAMELESS CITY.

IT'S A LONG
STORY HOW THOSE
JOURNALS FELL
INTO MY HANDS.

NONETHELESS... THE CITY HE SPOKE
OF IN THOSE STRANGE VERSES...

...THE CITY SEEN BY NO LIVING MAN...

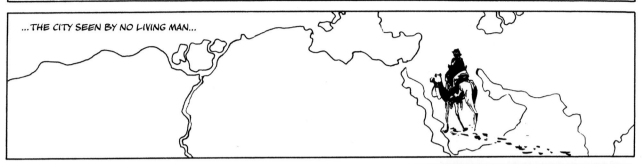

...IT CALLED TO ME LIKE A SIREN, DROWNING OUT THE
VOICE OF REASON BEGGING ME TO DESIST FROM THIS
TERRIBLE MADNESS. I DEFIED THAT VOICE...

AND AFTER COUNTLESS
UNFORESEEN OBSTACLES...

ASTRIDE MY CAMEL AT LAST I REACHED
THOSE UNTRODDEN RUINS.

IN AND OUT AMONGST THE SHAPELESS FOUNDATIONS OF HOUSES AND PALACES I WANDERED, FINDING NEVER A CARVING OR INSCRIPTION TO TELL OF THOSE MEN, IF MEN THEY WERE, WHO BUILT THE CITY AND DWELT THEREIN SO LONG AGO.

THE ONLY THING THAT CAUGHT MY EYE WERE SEVERAL SMALL, SAND-CHOKED APERTURES.

I CLEARED ONE WITH MY SPADE AND CRAWLED THROUGH IT, CARRYING A TORCH TO REVEAL WHATEVER MYSTERIES IT MIGHT HOLD.

AFTER SOME TIME, THE TUNNEL WIDENED ENOUGH THAT I COULD STAND QUITE UPRIGHT.

STRANGE THOUGHTS SWIRLED THROUGH MY MIND. IN SOME OF THE CORNERS I SAW STRANGE ALTARS AND STONES, SUGGESTING FORGOTTEN RITUALS OF A TERRIBLE, REPUGNANT, INEXPLICABLE WORLD.

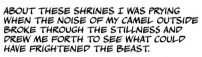

ABOUT THESE SHRINES I WAS PRYING WHEN THE NOISE OF MY CAMEL OUTSIDE BROKE THROUGH THE STILLNESS AND DREW ME FORTH TO SEE WHAT COULD HAVE FRIGHTENED THE BEAST.

I LOOKED SOUTH FROM WHENCE THE WIND WAS BLOWING AND MADE OUT A TEMPLE MUCH LARGER THAN THE ONES I HAD ALREADY SEEN; FROM ITS BLACK ORIFICE CAME THE UNCANNY SOUND THAT HAD FRIGHTENED MY CAMEL.

I PLODDED TOWARD THIS TEMPLE, DRAWN LIKE A MOTH TO A FLAME.

ITS DARK DOORWAY WAS FAR LESS CLOGGED WITH SAND, AND THE TERRIFIC FORCE OF THAT ICY WIND POURED MADLY OUT, SIGHING UNCANNILY AS IT SPREAD ABOUT THE WEIRD RUINS.

I WAS MORE AFRAID THAN I COULD EXPLAIN, YET I CROSSED INTO THE DARK CHAMBER.

THE LIGHT OF MY TORCH REVEALED A PATH THAT LED TO A DISTANT ABYSS, YET I HESITATED ONLY A MOMENT BEFORE COMMENCING TO CLIMB DOWN.

THE PASSAGE LED DOWN LIKE SOME HIDEOUS HAUNTED WELL, BRIMMING WITH DARKNESS AND MYSTERY.

OVER AND OVER I REPEATED A PHRASE OF LORD DUNSAY'S: "THE UNREVERBERATE BLACKNESS OF THE ABYSS."

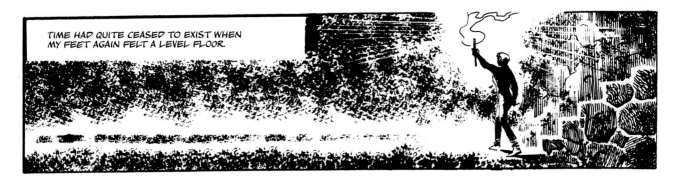

TIME HAD QUITE CEASED TO EXIST WHEN MY FEET AGAIN FELT A LEVEL FLOOR.

IT HAD BEEN SOME TIME SINCE MY TORCH HAD GONE OUT, AND ALL AT ONCE I REALIZED I COULD SEE THE DIM OUTLINES OF THE CORRIDOR, REVEALED BY SOME UNKNOWN SUBTERRANEAN PHOSPHORESCENCE.

I MADE OUT AN ENORMOUS WALL LINED WITH CASES OF WOOD HAVING GLASS FRONTS.

I APPROACHED ONE AND FOUND THAT IT CONTAINED THE MUMMIFIED FORM OF A CREATURE OUTREACHING IN GROTESQUENESS THE MOST CHAOTIC DREAMS OF MAN.

I CREPT FORWARD, BETWEEN ROWS OF BEINGS THAT REACHED OUT FOR ME. THIS CIVILIZATION HAD RISEN TO A HIGHER CULTURAL LEVEL THAN THOSE IMMEASURABLY LATER CIVILIZATIONS OF EGYPT AND CHALDAEA COULD EVEN HAVE DREAMED.

I MADE OUT A MURAL COVERED WITH STRANGE HIEROGLYPHICS. I SHUDDERED TO THINK THAT MINE WAS THE ONLY HUMAN FORM AMIDST THE MANY RELICS AND SYMBOLS OF PRIMORDIAL LIFE.

BUT THEN I SAW IT... ONE TERRIBLE FINAL SCENE SHOWED A PRIMITIVE-LOOKING MAN.

THE CASES SEEMED TO EMIT AN ANTIQUITY TOO REMOTE FOR CALCULATION.

DESPITE MY EXHAUSTION, I FOUND MYSELF FRANTICALLY LOOKING BACK...

...ALONG THE BLACK CORRIDOR TOWARD THE TUNNELS THAT ROSE TO THE OUTER WORLD.

THINKING OF THE MUMMIFIED CREATURES SO CLOSE TO ME, I FELT A NEW THROB OF TERROR.

THE SIGHT OF A BRASS DOOR BROUGHT ME TO MY SENSES AND SPURRED ME ONWARD.

I CREPT FORWARD SLOWLY, THEN FROZE, STUNNED.

INSTEAD OF OTHER ROOMS, BEFORE ME STRETCHED AN INFINITE SPACE OF SHINING MYSTERY.

A DOOR TO...

AN UNKNOWN DIMENSION!

THEN, IN THAT TOMB OF UNNUMBERED AEON-DEAD ANTIQUITIES, I HEARD THE GHASTLY CURSING AND SNARLING OF STRANGE-TONGUED FIENDS...

TURNING, I SAW OUTLINED AGAINST THE LUMINOUS AETHER OF THE ABYSS...

...RUSHING TOWARD THE DOOR, THOSE HATE-DISTORTED BEINGS, GROTESQUELY PANOPLIED, HALF-TRANSPARENT; DEVILS OF A RACE NO MAN MIGHT MISTAKE:

...A NIGHTMARE HORDE...

THE STRANGE CREATURES FROM THE GLASS CASES!

A MOMENT LATER,
A LOW MOAN AS OF A
DISTANT THRONG OF
CONDEMNED SPIRITS
CAME FROM THE
DOORWAY.

MORE AND MORE MADLY POURED THE
SHRIEKING, MOANING NIGHT-WIND INTO
THAT GULF OF THE INNER EARTH...

...I DROPPED PRONE AND CLUTCHED
VAINLY AT THE FLOOR...

...HORRIFIED TO FIND MYSELF SLIPPING
LITTLE BY LITTLE TOWARD THE DOOR...

...AND TOWARD THE PHOSPHORESCENT ABYSS THAT
SHONE MALIGNANTLY ON THE OTHER SIDE.

WHEN THE LAST OF THE CREATURES HAD PASSED, THE GREAT BRAZEN DOOR CLANGED SHUT WITH A DEAFENING PEAL OF METALLIC MUSIC.

AND AS THE WIND DIED AWAY, I WAS PLUNGED INTO THE GHOUL-PEOPLED BLACKNESS OF EARTH'S BOWELS.

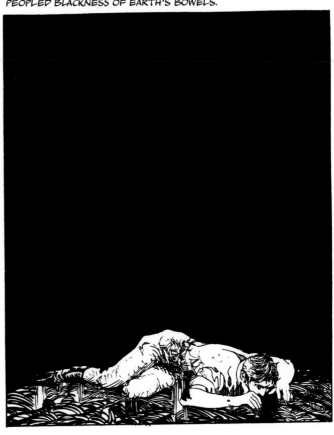

ONLY THE GRIM BROODING DESERT GODS KNOW WHAT REALLY TOOK PLACE—WHAT INDESCRIBABLE STRUGGLES AND SCRAMBLES IN THE DARK I ENDURED TO RETURN TO THE SURFACE...

...WHAT ABADDON GUIDED ME BACK TO LIFE?

I MUST ALWAYS REMEMBER AND SHIVER IN THE NIGHT-WIND...

TILL OBLIVION—OR WORSE—CLAIMS ME.

IS WHAT I SAW AN ANTECHAMBER TO THAT WHICH AWAITS US AFTER DEATH?

MONSTROUS, UNNATURAL, COLOSSAL, WAS THE THING—TOO FAR BEYOND ALL THE IDEAS OF MAN TO BE BELIEVED EXCEPT IN THE SILENT DAMNABLE SMALL HOURS WHEN ONE CANNOT SLEEP.

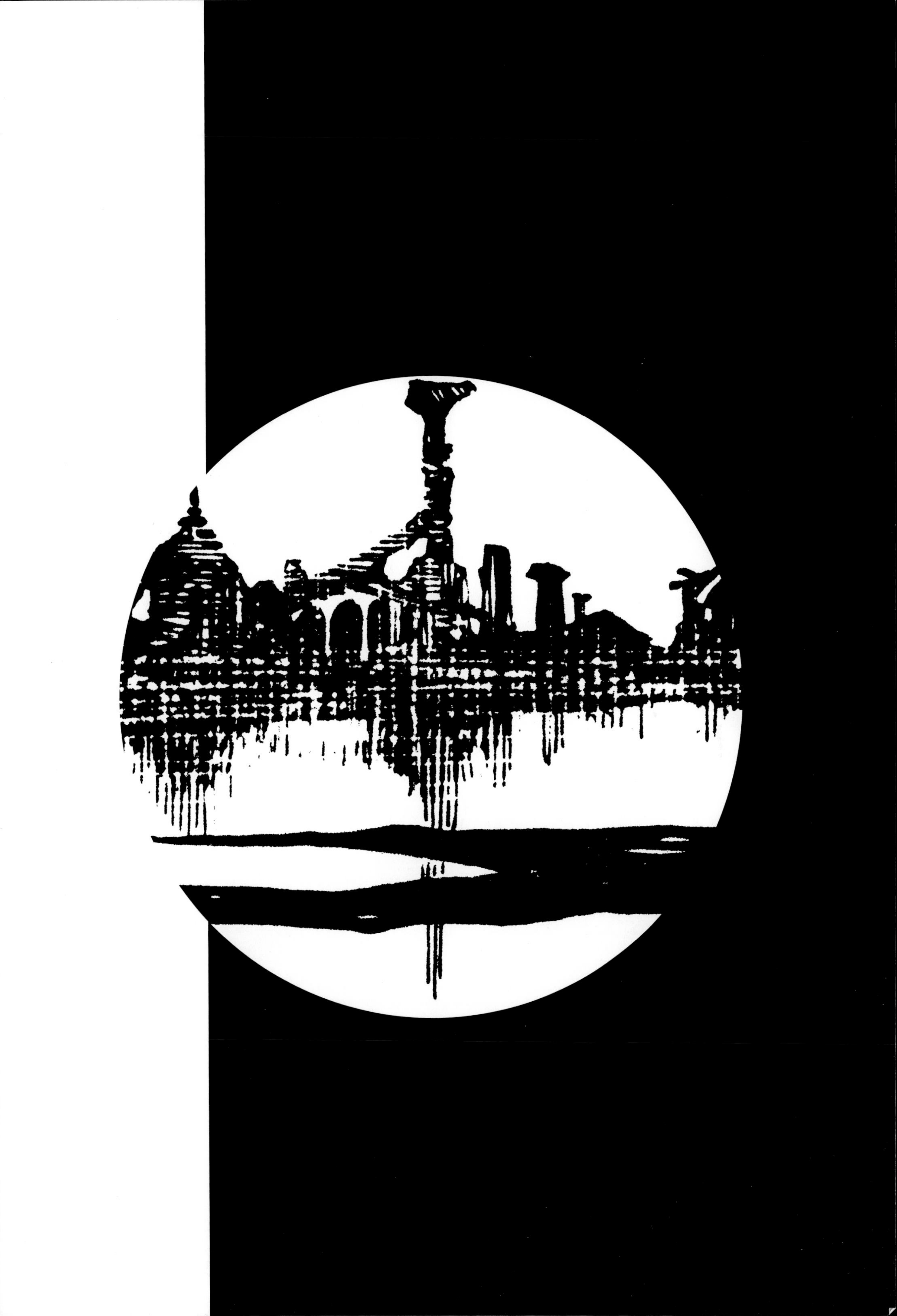

The Festival

"OF SUCH GREAT POWERS OR BEINGS THERE MAY BE CONCEIVABLY A SURVIVAL OF A HUGELY REMOTE PERIOD. . . FORMS OF WHICH POETRY AND LEGEND ALONE HAVE CAUGHT A FLYING MEMORY AND CALLED THEM GODS, MONSTERS, MYTHICAL BEINGS OF ALL SORTS AND KINDS. . ."

–ALGERNON BLACKWOOD

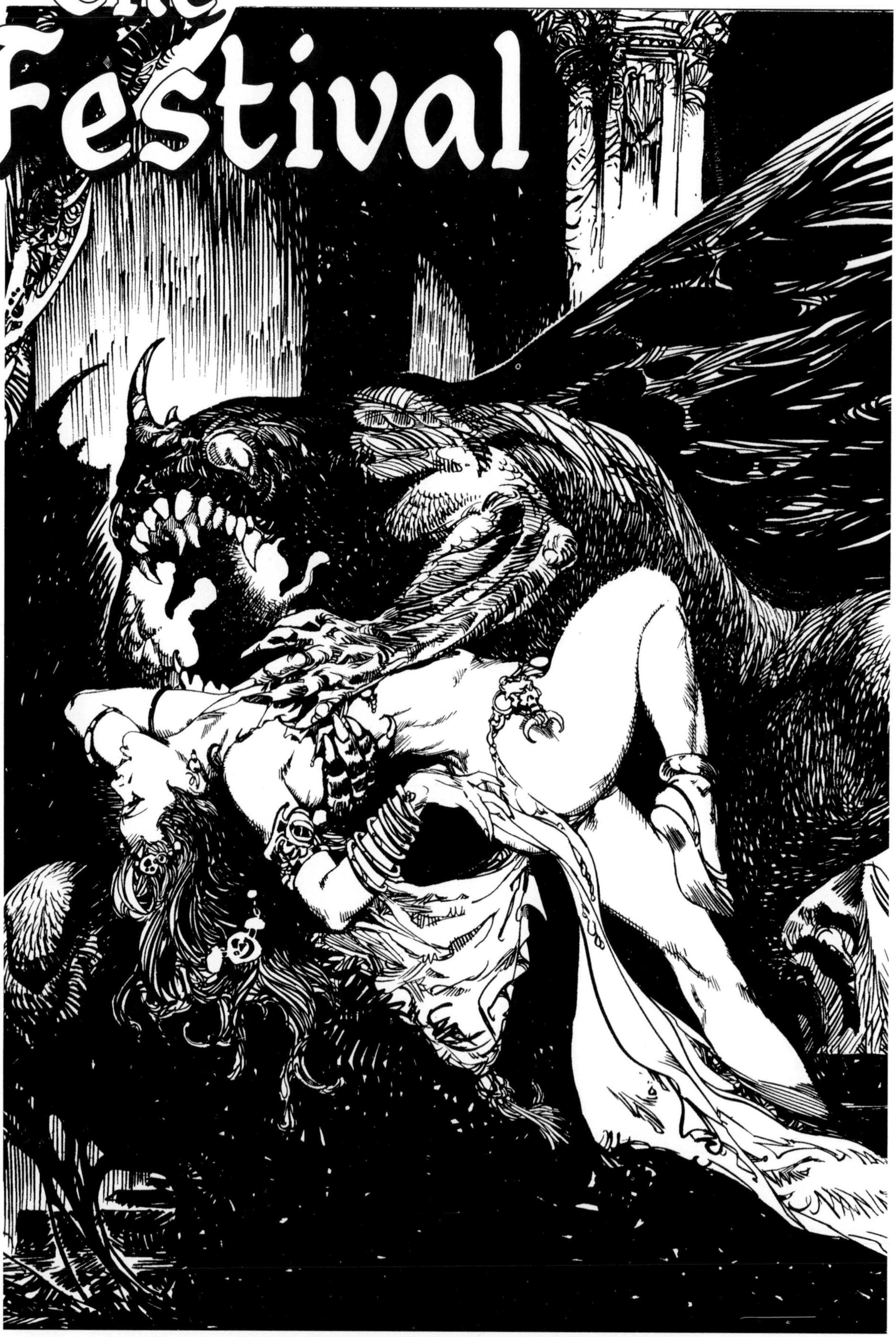

I WAS FAR FROM HOME, AND THE SPELL OF THE EASTERN SEA WAS UPON ME.

MY FATHERS HAD CALLED ME TO THE OLD TOWN BEYOND.

JUST OVER THE HILL WHERE THE TWISTING WILLOWS WRITHED AGAINST THE CLEARING SKY AND DISTANT STARS.

THERE LAY THE VERY ANCIENT TOWN I HAD NEVER SEEN BUT OFTEN DREAMED OF.

BEYOND THE HILL'S CREST I SAW KINGSPORT OUTSPREAD FROSTILY IN THE GLOAMING.

ANTIQUITY SEEMED TO HOVER ON GREY WINGS OVER WINTER-WHITENED GABLES AND ROOFS.

AND AGAINST THE ROTTING WHARVES THE SEA POUNDED; THE SEA OUT OF WHICH OUR PEOPLE HAD COME IN THE ELDER TIME.

IT WAS THE YULETIDE, THAT MEN CALL CHRISTMAS THOUGH THEY KNOW IN THEIR HEARTS IT IS OLDER THAN BETHLEHEM AND BABYLON, OLDER EVEN THAN MANKIND.

I HAD COME AT LAST TO THE ANCIENT TOWN WHERE MY PEOPLE COMMANDED THEIR SONS TO KEEP FESTIVAL...

...ONCE EVERY CENTURY, THAT THE MEMORY OF PRIMAL SECRETS MIGHT NOT BE FORGOTTEN.

SECRET, MYSTERIOUS RITUALS THAT NONE LIVING COULD UNDERSTAND.

I WAS THE ONLY ONE WHO CAME BACK THAT NIGHT TO THE OLD FISHING TOWN AS LEGEND BADE.

I PASSED A BURYING-GROUND WHERE BLACK GRAVESTONES STUCK GHOULISHLY THROUGH THE SNOW LIKE THE DECAYED FINGERNAILS OF A GIGANTIC CORPSE.

...AND SOMETIMES I THOUGHT I HEARD A DISTANT HORRIBLE CREAKING AS OF A GIBBET IN THE WIND.

THEY HAD HANGED FOUR KINSMEN OF MINE FOR WITCHCRAFT IN 1692...

I CEASED TO LOOK FOR OTHER WAYFARERS.

AND I ADVANCED THROUGH SHADOWY STONE WALLS.

THE SIGNS OF ANCIENT SHOPS AND SEA-TAVERNS CREAKED IN THE SALT BREEZE.

THE GROTESQUE DOOR KNOCKERS GLISTENED ALONG DESERTED LANES.

I WAS EAGER TO KNOCK AT THE DOOR OF MY PEOPLE. I'D BROUGHT A MAP OF THE CITY AND KNEW JUST WHERE IT SHOULD BE.

I HASTENED MY STEP AND AT LAST I REACHED...

THE SEVENTH HOUSE ON GREEN LANE, BUILT BEFORE 1650.

THE ARCHAIC IRON KNOCKER ECHOED IN THE QUEER SILENCE OF THAT AGED TOWN OF CURIOUS CUSTOMS...

...AND THE DOOR CREAKED OPEN.

I WAS AFRAID, BECAUSE I HAD NOT HEARD ANY FOOTSTEPS.

A BLAND-FACED OLD MAN BECKONED ME INSIDE, BUT SOMETHING IN HIS COUNTENANCE TERRIFIED ME.

THE EYES NEVER MOVED, AND THE SKIN WAS TOO MUCH LIKE WAX.

HE MADE SIGNS THAT HE WAS DUMB, THEN WROTE A QUAINT AND ANCIENT WELCOME WITH THE STYLUS AND WAX TABLET HE CARRIED.

THE PAST WAS VIVID THERE. AN INDEFINITE DAMPNESS SEEMED UPON THE PLACE, AND I MARVELLED THAT NO FIRE SHOULD BE BLAZING.

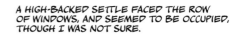

AT A SPINNING-WHEEL SAT A BENT OLD WOMAN, HER BACK TOWARD ME.

A HIGH-BACKED SETTLE FACED THE ROW OF WINDOWS, AND SEEMED TO BE OCCUPIED, THOUGH I WAS NOT SURE.

POINTING TO A CHAIR, TABLE, AND PILE OF BOOKS...

...THE OLD MAN NOW LEFT THE ROOM.

ONE BOOK CAUGHT MY EYE: THE UNMENTIONABLE NECRONOMICON OF THE MAD ARAB ABDUL ALHAZRED, A BOOK WHICH I HAD NEVER SEEN, BUT OF WHICH I HAD HEARD MONSTROUS THINGS WHISPERED.

I PLUNGED INTO MY READING. THE ONLY SOUNDS THAT BROKE THE SILENCE WERE THE MOANING OF THE WIND OUTSIDE, AND THE WHIR OF THE OLD WOMAN'S WHEEL.

WHEN ELEVEN STRUCK, THE OLD MAN CAME BACK.

HE WALKED TOWARD ME AND TOOK THE NECRO-NOMICON FROM MY HANDS.

HE DONNED A CLOAK, DRAPED ONE OVER THE WOMAN, AND THE TWO STARTED FOR THE OUTER DOOR.

HE BECKONED ME AS HE DREW HIS HOOD OVER THAT UNMOVING FACE... OR MASK.

WE WENT OUT INTO THE STREET, WHERE OTHER CLOAKED FIGURES POURED SILENTLY FROM EVERY DOORWAY...

...FORMING A MONSTROUS PROCESSION UP THE STREET.

I FOLLOWED MY VOICELESS GUIDE AMID THE SILENT CROWD; BUT SEEING NEVER A FACE AND HEARING NEVER A WORD.

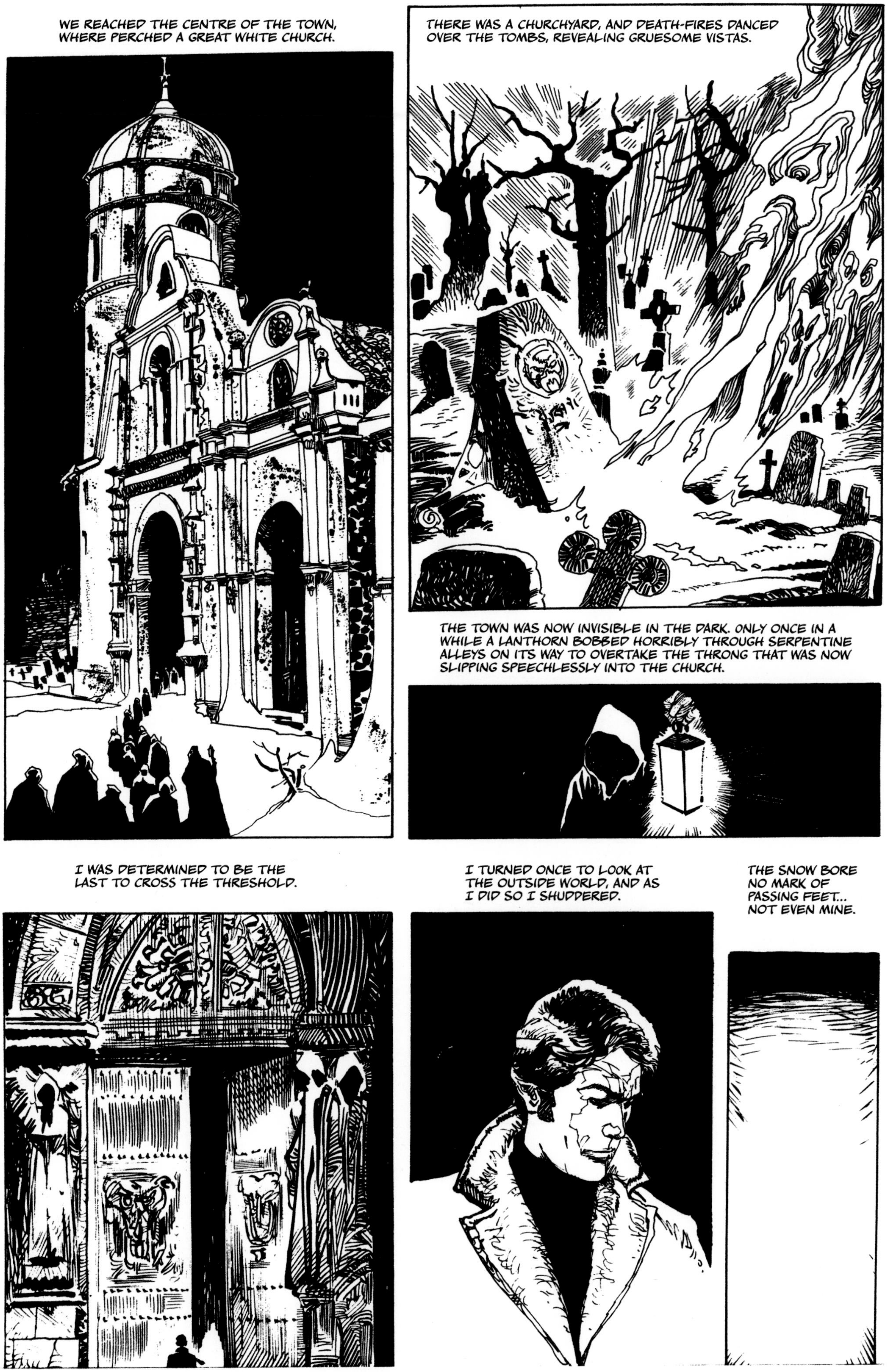
WE REACHED THE CENTRE OF THE TOWN, WHERE PERCHED A GREAT WHITE CHURCH.
THERE WAS A CHURCHYARD, AND DEATH-FIRES DANCED OVER THE TOMBS, REVEALING GRUESOME VISTAS.
THE TOWN WAS NOW INVISIBLE IN THE DARK. ONLY ONCE IN A WHILE A LANTHORN BOBBED HORRIBLY THROUGH SERPENTINE ALLEYS ON ITS WAY TO OVERTAKE THE THRONG THAT WAS NOW SLIPPING SPEECHLESSLY INTO THE CHURCH.
I WAS DETERMINED TO BE THE LAST TO CROSS THE THRESHOLD.
I TURNED ONCE TO LOOK AT THE OUTSIDE WORLD, AND AS I DID SO I SHUDDERED.
THE SNOW BORE NO MARK OF PASSING FEET... NOT EVEN MINE.

THE CHURCH WAS SCARCE LIGHTED BY ALL THE LANTERNS THAT HAD ENTERED IT...

...FOR MOST OF THE THRONG HAD ALREADY VANISHED THROUGH A TRAP-DOOR JUST BEFORE THE PULPIT.

I FOLLOWED DUMBLY DOWN THE FOOTWORN STEPS AND INTO THE DANK, SUFFOCATING CRYPT.

IT WAS A SILENT, SHOCKING DESCENT.

THE TOMB'S FLOOR HAD ANOTHER APERTURE.

AND A MOMENT LATER, I FOUND MYSELF DESCENDING A SPIRAL STAIRCASE THAT WOUND ENDLESSLY DOWN INTO THE BOWELS OF THE EARTH.

WHAT MAINLY TROUBLED ME WAS THAT THE MYRIAD FOOTFALLS MADE NO SOUND AND SET UP NO ECHOES.

THE PUNGENT ODOR OF DECAY COMING FROM THE WALLS GREW QUITE UNBEARABLE.

AFTER MORE AEONS OF DESCENT, WE REACHED SOME SIDE PASSAGES OR BURROWS LIKE IMPIOUS CATACOMBS OF NAMELESS MENACE.

I SHIVERED THAT A TOWN SHOULD BE SO AGED AND MAGGOTY WITH SUBTERRANEOUS EVIL.

I DID NOT LIKE THE THINGS THAT THE NIGHT HAD BROUGHT, AND WISHED BITTERLY THAT NO FOREFATHER HAD SUMMONED ME TO THIS PRIMAL RITE.

AT LAST I HEARD ANOTHER SOUND: THE THIN, WHINING MOCKERY OF A FEEBLE FLUTE.

SUDDENLY THERE SPREAD OUT BEFORE ME THE BOUNDLESS VISTA OF AN INNER WORLD.

THE CLOAKED THRONGS HAD FORMED A SEMICIRCLE AROUND A COLUMN OF GREENISH FLAME THAT EMANATED FROM ONE OF THE FRIGHTFUL ABYSSES.

IT WAS THE **RITE OF WINTER,** OLDER THAN MAN.

THE PRIMAL RITE OF SPRING'S PROMISE BEYOND THE SNOWS.

I SAW SOMETHING AMORPHOUSLY SQUATTED FAR AWAY FROM THE LIGHT, PIPING NOISOMELY ON A FLUTE.

BEFORE THE FIRE, A BRAZIER EMITTED A YELLOW SMOKE THAT COILED AROUND THE FLAME LIKE A COLOSSAL SERPENT.

SUDDENLY A NAKED WOMAN LEAPT BETWEEN THE CROWD AND THE BRAZIER, HER EYES BLAZING, HER LONG, TANGLED HAIR FLYING IN ALL DIRECTIONS AS SHE DANCED GIDDILY.

UNTIL SHE FELL, PROSTRATING HERSELF BEFORE THE COLUMN OF FLAME.

IMMEDIATELY THERE AROSE A FANTASTICAL FIGURE, A CONVERGENCE OF HUMAN AND BESTIAL ELEMENTS.

IN ITS HAND WAS A FIR BRANCH, WHICH IT SWUNG LIKE A SWITCH.

THE CROWD BEGAN TO SHAKE THEIR ARMS TOWARD THE HALF-SEEN FLUTE-PLAYER.

THE GROTESQUE FIGURE APPROACHED THE WOMAN AND BEGAN TO FLOG HER WITH THE SWITCH.

THEN SHE LEAPT UP ONCE MORE AND SURRENDERED TO THE MOST INCREDIBLE AND SAVAGE DANCING THAT EVER I HAVE SEEN.

HER TORTURER DANCED ALONG WITH HER, KEEPING TIME, LETTING FLY THE LASH AGAINST HER NAKED SKIN.

THE MADNESS IN THE WOMAN'S EYES GREW... THAT RITUAL DANCE TURNING EVEN MORE SAVAGE AND FRENETIC.

BLOOD RAN DOWN ALL HER LIMBS, BUT THIS SEEMED ONLY TO SPUR ON HER WILD MOVEMENTS.

AT THE HEIGHT OF HER DELIRIUM, SHE FELL TO THE GROUND SHUDDERING AND GASPING, OVERCOME BY THE STRAIN.

THE SINISTER FIGURE WENT ON FLOGGING HER BODY AS SHE DRAGGED IT ACROSS THE GROUND, LEAVING A TRAIL OF STICKY BLOOD UP TO THE COLUMN OF FIRE.

THE EXECUTIONER NOW THREW THE BLOOD-SPATTERED SWITCH INTO THE DARKNESS...

...LIFTED UP THE VICTIM IN HIS POWERFUL ARMS AND, WITH A BLIND, BESTIAL PASSION...

...HURLED HER TOWARD THE FIRE, WHICH TOOK HER LIFE IN A RAIN OF SPARKS LIKE A PROFANE, DELIRIOUS ACT OF WORSHIP.

THE MAN WHO HAD BROUGHT ME MADE STIFF CEREMONIAL MOTIONS TO THE CLOAKED SEMICIRCLE.

AND THEY DID GROVELLING OBEISANCE WHEN HE HELD ABOVE HIS HEAD THAT ABHORRENT *NECRONOMICON*.

NECRONOMICON

THE COLUMN OF FLAME WENT OUT AND THE
SMOKE FROM THE BRAZIER TURNED REDDISH.

THE OLD MAN MADE A SIGNAL TO THE
FLUTE-PLAYER IN THE DARKNESS...

...AND HE THEREUPON CHANGED ITS FEEBLE
DRONE TO A SCARCE LOUDER ONE.

OUT OF THE UNIMAGINABLE BLACKNESS BEYOND WHICH THE FLAME HAD GONE CAME THE BEATING OF WINGS.

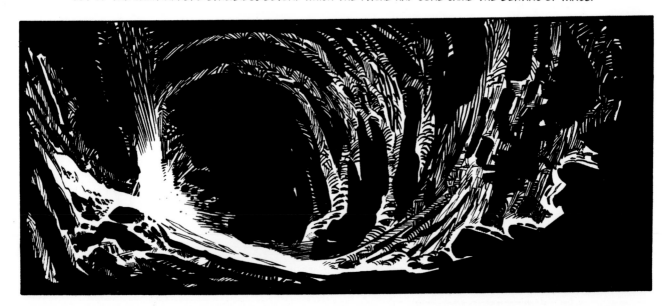

A HORDE HYBRID OF WINGED THINGS CAME TOWARD US.

THEY LANDED ON THE FLOOR AND FLOPPED LIMPLY ALONG.

THE COWLED FIGURES MOUNTED THEM...

...AND RODE OFF ALONG THE REACHES OF THAT UNLIGHTED RIVER.

THE OLD SPINNING WOMAN HAD GONE WITH THE THRONG.

ONLY I AND THE OLD MAN REMAINED.

I REFUSED TO MOUNT ONE OF THE LAST TWO BEASTS.

IN HIS PECULIAR LANGUAGE, THE OLD MAN WROTE THAT THE MOST SECRET MYSTERIES WERE YET TO BE PERFORMED.

HE WAS THE TRUE DEPUTY OF MY FATHERS.

HE PULLED FROM HIS LOOSE ROBE A SEAL RING AND A WATCH, BOTH WITH MY FAMILY ARMS.

BUT IT WAS A HIDEOUS PROOF, BECAUSE I KNEW FROM OLD PAPERS THAT THE WATCH HAD BEEN BURIED WITH MY GREAT-GREAT-GREAT-GREAT-GRANDFATHER IN 1698.

THE OLD MAN DREW BACK HIS HOOD...

...AND POINTED TO THE FAMILY RESEMBLANCE IN HIS FACE...

...BUT I ONLY SHUDDERED, BECAUSE I WAS SURE THAT THE FACE WAS MERELY A DEVILISH WAXEN MASK.

I REALIZED THE OLD MAN WAS RUNNING OUT OF PATIENCE.

THE FLOPPING ANIMALS WERE NOW SCRATCHING RESTLESSLY AT THE LICHENS.

WHEN ONE OF THE THINGS BEGAN TO WADDLE AWAY...

...HE TURNED QUICKLY TO STOP IT.

HIS SUDDEN MOTION DISLODGED THE WAXEN MASK FROM WHAT SHOULD HAVE BEEN HIS HEAD.

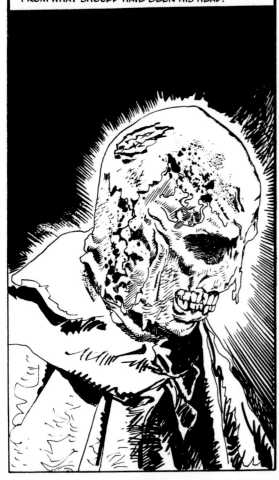

REVEALING THE MOST TERRIFYING NIGHTMARE THAT HUMAN EYES HAVE EVER WITNESSED!

BEFORE THE MADNESS OF MY SCREAMS COULD BRING DOWN UPON ME ALL THE CHARNEL LEGIONS THESE PEST-GULFS MIGHT CONCEAL...

...THE DARKNESS SWALLOWED ME AS IF I'D FLUNG MYSELF INTO THAT OILY UNDERGROUND RIVER...

AT THE HOSPITAL THEY TOLD ME I HAD BEEN FOUND IN KINGSPORT HARBOUR.

BUT THE CITY I FOUND MYSELF IN HAD NOTHING TO DO WITH WHAT I HAD WITNESSED THE NIGHT BEFORE. MY HEAD WAS SPINNING.

APPARENTLY I'D GOTTEN LOST ALONG THE CLIFFS AT ORANGE POINT.

FROM THEN ON, MY DREAMS WERE TERRIFYING, INSPIRED BY SOME FRAGMENTS I'D READ IN THE *NECRONOMICON*.

THEY HAMMERED IN MY HEAD, FORGING THE MOST HORRIBLE NIGHTMARES.

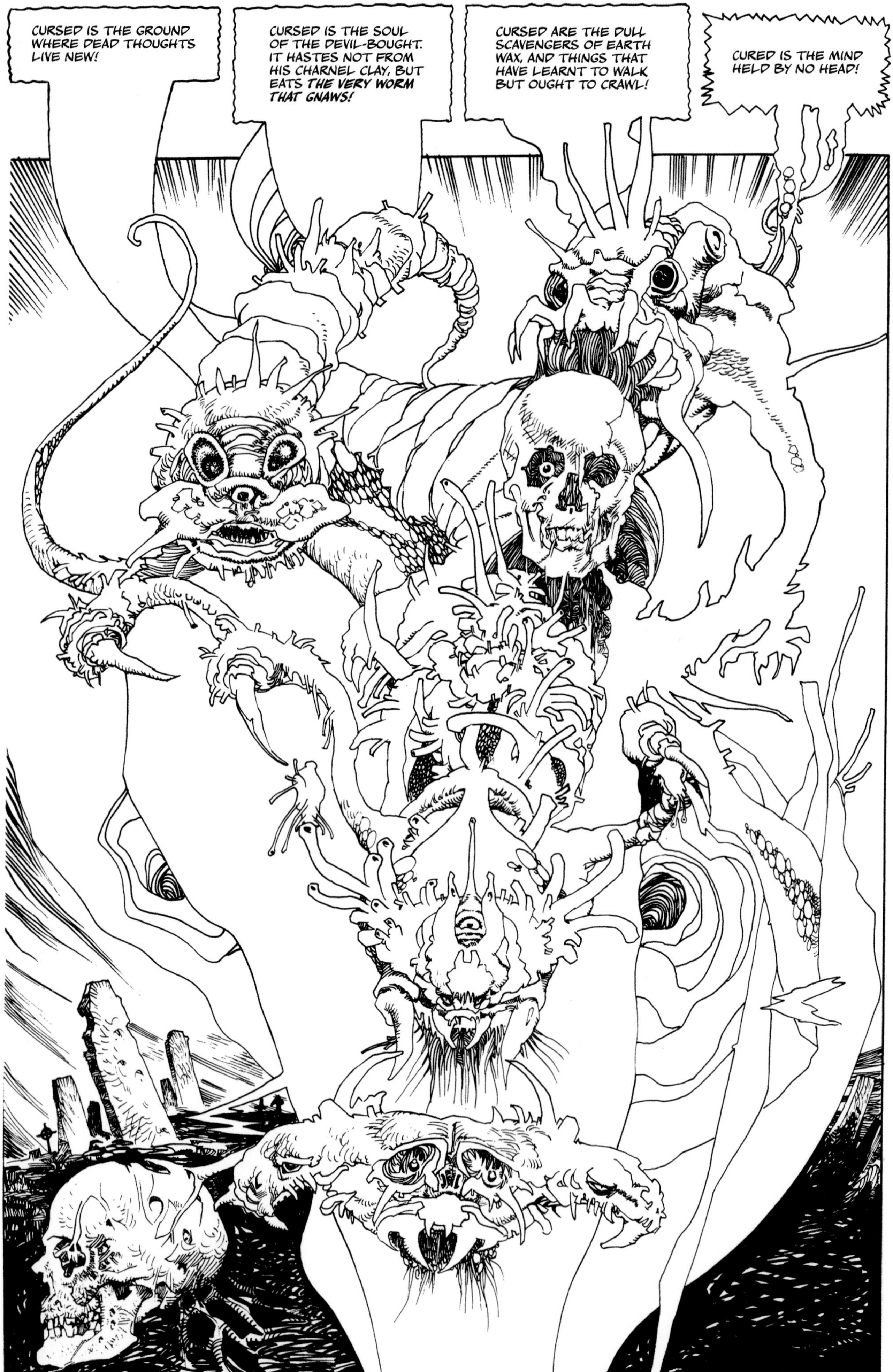
CURSED IS THE GROUND WHERE DEAD THOUGHTS LIVE NEW!
CURSED IS THE SOUL OF THE DEVIL-BOUGHT. IT HASTES NOT FROM HIS CHARNEL CLAY, BUT EATS ***THE VERY WORM THAT GNAWS!***
CURSED ARE THE DULL SCAVENGERS OF EARTH WAX, AND THINGS THAT HAVE LEARNT TO WALK BUT OUGHT TO CRAWL!
CURED IS THE MIND HELD BY NO HEAD!

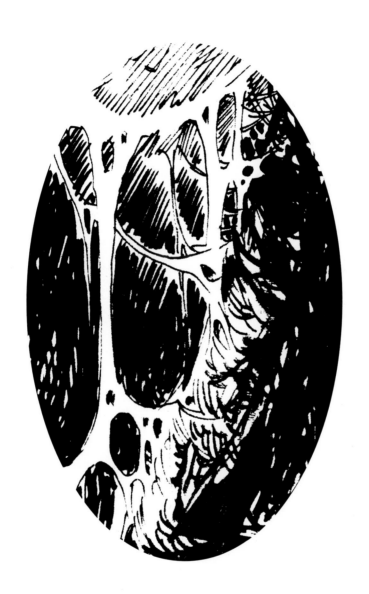

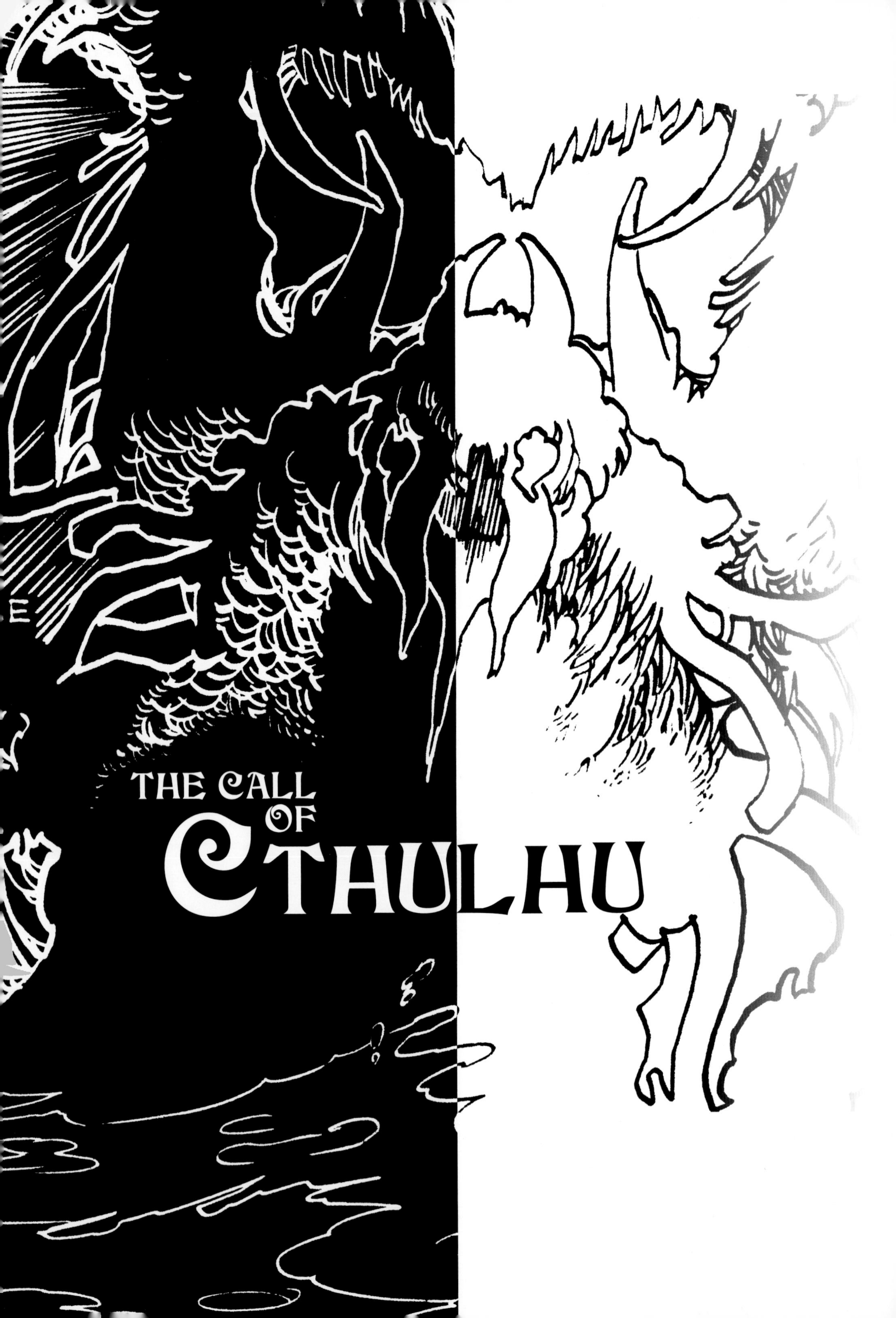
THE CALL OF
CTHULHU

THE HORROR IN CLAY

"WE LIVE ON A PLACID ISLAND OF IGNORANCE IN THE MIDST OF BLACK SEAS OF INFINITY, AND IT WAS NOT MEANT THAT WE SHOULD VOYAGE FAR."

MY KNOWLEDGE OF THE THING BEGAN IN THE WINTER OF 1926-27 WITH THE DEATH OF MY GRAND-UNCLE GEORGE GAMMELL ANGELL.

HE WAS PROFESSOR EMERITUS OF SEMITIC LANGUAGES AT BROWN UNIVERSITY, PROVIDENCE, RHODE ISLAND, AND WIDELY KNOWN AS AN AUTHORITY ON ANCIENT INSCRIPTIONS.

HE HAD FREQUENTLY BEEN RESORTED TO BY THE HEADS OF PROMINENT UNIVERSITIES AROUND THE WORLD.

THE PROFESSOR HAD BEEN STRICKEN WHILST RETURNING FROM THE NEWPORT BOAT. INTEREST WAS INTENSIFIED BY THE OBSCURITY OF THE CAUSE OF DEATH.

HE'D FALLEN SUDDENLY AFTER HAVING BEEN JOSTLED BY A NAUTICAL-LOOKING NEGRO WHO HAD COME FROM ONE OF THE WRETCHED TAVERNS ALONG THE DOCKS.

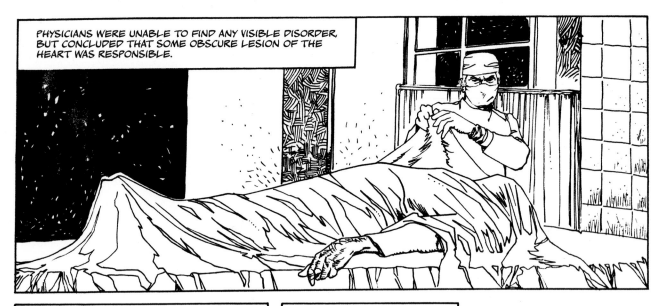

PHYSICIANS WERE UNABLE TO FIND ANY VISIBLE DISORDER, BUT CONCLUDED THAT SOME OBSCURE LESION OF THE HEART WAS RESPONSIBLE.

AT THE TIME I SAW NO REASON TO DISSENT FROM THIS DICTUM, BUT LATTERLY I AM INCLINED TO WONDER...

AS MY GRAND-UNCLE'S ONLY HEIR, I WAS EXPECTED TO GO OVER HIS PAPERS WITH SOME THOROUGHNESS, SO I MOVED HIS FILES AND BOXES TO MY QUARTERS IN BOSTON.

MUCH OF THE MATERIAL WHICH I CORRELATED WILL BE LATER PUBLISHED BY THE AMERICAN ARCHAEOLOGICAL SOCIETY, BUT THERE WAS ONE BOX WHICH I FOUND EXCEEDINGLY PUZZLING.

I DID NOT FIND THE KEY TILL IT OCCURRED TO ME TO EXAMINE THE PERSONAL RING WHICH THE PROFESSOR CARRIED ALWAYS.

INSIDE, I FOUND A QUEER CLAY BAS-RELIEF AND SOME DISJOINTED JOTTINGS AND CUTTINGS.

THE BAS-RELIEF WAS A ROUGH RECTANGLE LESS THAN AN INCH THICK AND ABOUT FIVE BY SIX INCHES IN AREA; OBVIOUSLY OF MODERN ORIGIN. ITS DESIGNS, HOWEVER, SUGGESTED ANTIQUITY, EVEN PREHISTORY.

I FAILED TO IDENTIFY THIS PARTICULAR SPECIES OF WRITING, OR EVEN TO HINT AT ITS REMOTEST AFFILIATIONS.

ABOVE THESE HIEROGLYPHICS WAS A FIGURE WHICH ONLY A DISEASED FANCY COULD CONCEIVE.

BEHIND THE FIGURE WAS A VAGUE SUGGESTION OF A CYCLOPEAN ARCHITECTURAL BACKGROUND.

SOME PAPERS WRITTEN BY MY UNCLE SAT ASIDE A STACK OF PRESS CUTTINGS.

THE MAIN DOCUMENT WAS HEADED

CTHULHU CULT

THE OTHERS WERE ALL BRIEF NOTES: ACCOUNTS OF THE QUEER DREAMS OF DIFFERENT PERSONS, CITATIONS FROM THEOSOPHICAL BOOKS (NOTABLY W. SCOTT-ELLIOT'S *ATLANTIS AND THE LOST LEMURIA*), AND SUCH MYTHOLOGICAL AND ANTHROPOLOGICAL SOURCE-BOOKS AS FRAZER'S *GOLDEN BOUGH* AND MISS MURRAY'S *WITCH-CULT IN WESTERN EUROPE.*

THE CUTTINGS LARGELY ALLUDED TO OUTRÉ MENTAL ILLNESSES AND OUTBREAKS OF GROUP FOLLY OR MANIA IN THE SPRING OF 1925.

THE FIRST HALF OF THE PRINCIPAL MANUSCRIPT TOLD THE TALE OF HENRY ANTHONY WILCOX, WHO, ON MARCH 1ST, 1925, HAD CALLED UPON MY UNCLE BEARING THE SINGULAR CLAY BAS-RELIEF, WHICH WAS THEN EXCEEDINGLY DAMP AND FRESH.

WILCOX WAS A YOUNG SCULPTOR OF KNOWN GENIUS WHO HAD FROM CHILDHOOD EXCITED ATTENTION THROUGH THE STRANGE STORIES AND ODD DREAMS HE WAS IN THE HABIT OF RELATING. HE CALLED HIMSELF "PSYCHICALLY HYPERSENSITIVE."

HE WAS QUITE AGITATED AND ABRUPTLY ASKED FOR THE BENEFIT OF HIS HOST'S ARCHAEOLOGICAL KNOWLEDGE IN IDENTIFYING THE HIEROGLYPHICS ON THE BAS-RELIEF.

MY UNCLE SHEWED SOME SHARPNESS IN REPLYING, FOR THE CONSPICUOUS FRESHNESS OF THE TABLET IMPLIED KINSHIP WITH ANYTHING BUT ARCHAEOLOGY.

YOUNG WILCOX'S REJOINDER IMPRESSED MY UNCLE.

HE SAID, "IT IS NEW, INDEED, FOR I MADE IT LAST NIGHT IN A DREAM OF STRANGE CITIES; AND DREAMS ARE OLDER THAN BROODING TYRE, OR THE CONTEMPLATIVE SPHINX, OR GARDEN-GIRDLED BABYLON."

IT WAS THEN HE BEGAN TO RELATE HIS DREAM, WINNING THE INTEREST OF MY UNCLE.

THERE HAD BEEN A SLIGHT EARTHQUAKE TREMOR THE NIGHT BEFORE, THE MOST CONSIDERABLE FELT IN NEW ENGLAND FOR SOME YEARS, AFTER WHICH HE'D FALLEN ASLEEP...

RUUUMMMBLEE...

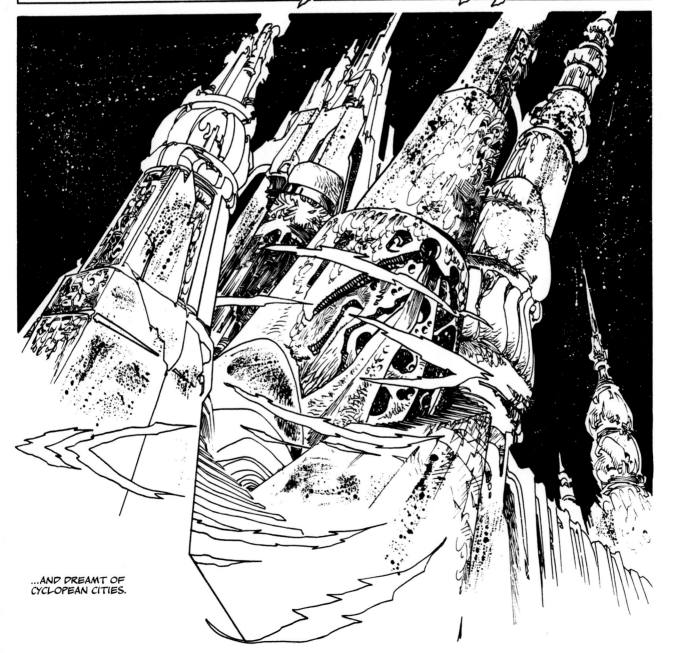

...AND DREAMT OF CYCLOPEAN CITIES.

FILLED WITH SKY-FLUNG MONOLITHS...   ...ALL DRIPPING WITH GREEN OOZE...   ...AND SINISTER WITH LATENT HORROR.

HIEROGLYPHICS AND STRANGE FIGURES HAD COVERED THE WALLS AND PILLARS.

AND FROM SOME UNDETERMINED POINT BELOW HAD COME A CHAOTIC SENSATION WHICH ONLY FANCY COULD TRANSMUTE INTO SOUND, BUT WHICH HE ATTEMPTED TO RENDER BY THE ALMOST UNPRONOUNCEABLE JUMBLE OF LETTERS, *"CTHULHU FHTAGN"*

PROFESSOR ANGELL QUESTIONED THE SCULPTOR WITH SCIENTIFIC MINUTENESS.

BUT HE WAS CONNECTED WITH NO STRANGE CULTS OR SOCIETIES, NOR A MEMBER OF SOME MYSTICAL OR PAGANLY RELIGIOUS BODY.

WHEN PROFESSOR ANGELL BECAME CONVINCED THAT THE SCULPTOR WAS IGNORANT OF ANY CULT OR SYSTEM OF CRYPTIC LORE, HE ASKED HIS VISITOR FOR FUTURE REPORTS OF DREAMS.

THE YOUNG MAN AGREED, AND FROM THEN ON, HE CALLED REGULARLY.

ALWAYS TELLING OF THE SAME DREAMS.

THE TERRIBLE CYCLOPEAN VISTAS OF DARK AND DRIPPING STONE.

THE DISTRESS OF THE SUBTERRENE VOICE SHOUTING MONOTONOUSLY IN ENIGMATICAL SENSE-IMPACTS INSCRIBABLE AS...

AT SOME POINT, WILCOX FAILED TO APPEAR. INQUIRIES AT HIS QUARTERS REVEALED THAT HE HAD BEEN STRICKEN WITH AN OBSCURE SORT OF FEVER AND TAKEN TO THE HOME OF HIS FAMILY.

HE HAD CRIED OUT IN THE NIGHT, AND HAD MANIFESTED SINCE THEN ONLY ALTERNATIONS OF UNCONSCIOUSNESS AND DELIRIUM.

MY UNCLE KEPT CLOSE WATCH OF THE CASE; CALLING OFTEN AT THE OFFICE OF THE DOCTOR IN CHARGE.

THE NIGHTMARES CONTINUED, NOW WITH A NEW ELEMENT ADDED.

A GIGANTIC THING "MILES HIGH" WHICH WALKED OR LUMBERED ABOUT.

IT MUST BE IDENTICAL WITH THE NAMELESS MONSTROSITY HE HAD SOUGHT TO DEPICT IN HIS DREAM-SCULPTURE.

ON APRIL 2ND, WILCOX SAT UPRIGHT IN BED. EVERY TRACE OF HIS MALADY SUDDENLY CEASED, HE REMEMBERED NOTHING OF HIS DREAMS, AND HE WISHED TO RETURN HOME IMMEDIATELY.

THIS CASE WOULD HAVE MEANT NO MORE TO MY UNCLE IF NOT FOR THE MANY OTHERS WHO CONSULTED WITH HIM ABOUT THEIR STRANGE DREAMS, ALL COINCIDING WITH THE PERIOD OF YOUNG WILCOX'S DELIRIUM.

A FOURTH REPORTED SCENES AND HALF-SOUNDS NOT UNLIKE THOSE WHICH WILCOX HAD DESCRIBED.

HALF CONFESSED TO FEELING ACUTE FEAR BEFORE THE GIGANTIC NAMELESS THING.

IN ONE CASE, WHICH THE NOTE DESCRIBES WITH EMPHASIS, AN ARCHITECT WITH LEANINGS TOWARD OCCULTISM WENT VIOLENTLY INSANE ON THE DATE OF YOUNG WILCOX'S SEIZURE.

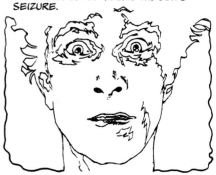

HE EXPIRED SEVERAL MONTHS LATER AFTER INCESSANT SCREAMINGS TO BE SAVED FROM SOME ESCAPED DENIZEN OF HELL.

I HAVE OFTEN WONDERED IF ALL THE OBJECTS OF THE PROFESSOR'S QUESTIONING FELT AS PUZZLED AS I.

THE PRESS CUTTINGS THAT MOST CAUGHT MY ATTENTION SPOKE OF:

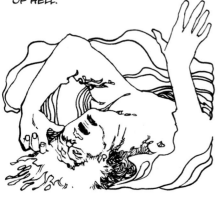

A THEOSOPHIST COLONY AS DONNING WHITE ROBES EN MASSE FOR SOME "GLORIOUS FULFILMENT" SOON TO ARRIVE...

VOODOO ORGIES MULTIPLYING IN HAYTI...

AND NEW YORK POLICEMEN MOBBED BY HYSTERICAL LEVANTINES ON THE NIGHT OF MARCH 22-23.

SO NUMEROUS WERE THE RECORDED TROUBLES IN INSANE ASYLUMS, THAT ONLY A MIRACLE CAN HAVE STOPPED THE MEDICAL FRATERNITY FROM NOTING STRANGE PARALLELISMS.

THE OLDER MATTERS WHICH HAD MADE THE SCULPTOR'S DREAM SO SIGNIFICANT TO MY UNCLE FORMED THE SUBJECT OF THE SECOND HALF OF HIS LONG MANUSCRIPT. HE HAD TITLED IT:

THE TALE OF INSPECTOR LEGRASSE

THE EXPERIENCE HAD COME IN 1908, WHEN THE AMERICAN ARCHAEOLOGICAL SOCIETY HELD ITS ANNUAL MEETING IN ST. LOUIS.

A MAN HAD APPROACHED MY UNCLE BEARING A STONE STATUETTE.

HIS NAME WAS JOHN RAYMOND LEGRASSE, AND HE WAS A POLICE INSPECTOR.

THE STATUETTE WAS GROTESQUE, REPULSIVE, AND APPARENTLY VERY ANCIENT, THOUGH HE WAS AT A LOSS TO DETERMINE ITS ORIGIN.

THE STATUETTE, IDOL, FETISH, OR WHATEVER IT WAS, HAD BEEN CAPTURED IN NEW ORLEANS DURING A RAID ON A SUPPOSED VOODOO MEETING.

SO SINGULAR AND HIDEOUS WERE THE RITES THAT THE POLICE COULD NOT BUT REALIZE THAT THEY HAD STUMBLED ON A DARK CULT TOTALLY UNKNOWN TO THEM.

OF ITS ORIGIN, APART FROM THE ERRATIC TALES EXTORTED FROM THE CAPTURED MEMBERS, NOTHING WAS TO BE DISCOVERED.

HENCE THE POLICE HAD DECIDED TO SEEK OUT ARCHAEOLOGISTS WHO COULD HELP TRACK THE CULT TO ITS FOUNTAIN-HEAD.

THE FIGURE WAS PASSED SLOWLY FROM MAN TO MAN FOR CLOSE AND CAREFUL STUDY.

THE ASPECT OF THE WHOLE WAS ABNORMALLY LIFE-LIKE, AND THE MORE SUBTLY FEARFUL.

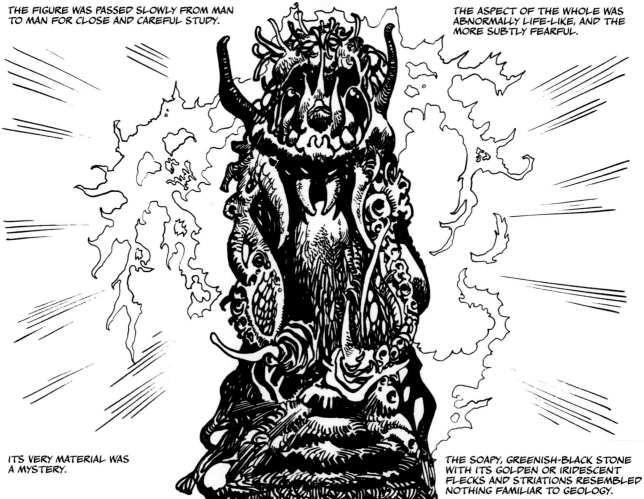

ITS VERY MATERIAL WAS A MYSTERY.

THE SOAPY, GREENISH-BLACK STONE WITH ITS GOLDEN OR IRIDESCENT FLECKS AND STRIATIONS RESEMBLED NOTHING FAMILIAR TO GEOLOGY.

YET THERE WAS ONE MAN IN THAT GATHERING, PROFESSOR WEBB, WHO SUSPECTED A TOUCH OF FAMILIARITY. HE HAD ONCE INVESTIGATED A TRIBE OF ESQUIMAUX IN GREENLAND.

THEIR RELIGION, A CURIOUS FORM OF DEVIL-WORSHIP, CHILLED HIM WITH ITS DELIBERATE BLOODTHIRSTINESS.

THEY'D HAD A FETISH OR *TORNASUK* THAT HAD COME DOWN FROM HORRIBLY ANCIENT AEONS...

...AROUND WHICH THEY MADE THEIR HUMAN SACRIFICES WHEN THE AURORA LEAPED HIGH OVER THE ICE CLIFFS.

SO FAR AS WEBB COULD TELL, THAT IDOL WAS A ROUGH PARALLEL IN ALL ESSENTIAL FEATURES OF THE BESTIAL THING NOW LYING BEFORE HIM.

THIS DATA WAS RECEIVED WITH EXCITEMENT BY INSPECTOR LEGRASSE, AND HE BEGAN AT ONCE TO PLY HIS INFORMANT WITH QUESTIONS.

THEN THEY COMPARED THE TWO CULTS SO MANY WORLDS APART.

THE PROFESSOR HAD TAKEN DOWN THE ESQUIMAUX'S CHANT AND IT SOUNDED LIKE: *"PH'NGLUI MGLW'NAFH CTHULHU R'LYEH WGAH'NAGL FHTAGN."*

LEGRASSE HAD BEEN LUCKIER WITH HIS PRISONERS AND KNEW THE TEXT MEANT SOMETHING LIKE THIS: "IN HIS HOUSE AT R'LYEH DEAD CTHULHU WAITS DREAMING."

AND NOW, IN RESPONSE TO A GENERAL AND URGENT DEMAND, INSPECTOR LEGRASSE RELATED AS FULLY AS POSSIBLE HIS EXPERIENCE WITH THE SWAMP WORSHIPPERS.

ON NOVEMBER 1ST, 1907, HE'D RECEIVED A SUMMONS FROM THE SWAMP. THE SQUATTERS WERE IN THE GRIP OF TERROR.

AN UNKNOWN THING HAD STOLEN UPON THEM IN THE NIGHT.

IT WAS VOODOO, BUT VOODOO OF A MORE TERRIBLE SORT THAN THEY HAD EVER KNOWN.

A MALEVOLENT TOM-TOM HAD BEGUN ITS INCESSANT BEATING IN THE HEART OF THE SWAMP WHERE NO DWELLER VENTURED.

SOME OF THEIR WOMEN AND CHILDREN HAD DISAPPEARED.

THEY HEARD INSANE SHOUTS, HARROWING SCREAMS, AND SOUL-CHILLING CHANTS.

SO A GROUP OF POLICE, FILLING VARIOUS VEHICLES, HAD SET OUT WITH THE SHIVERING SQUATTER AS A GUIDE.

AT THE END OF THE PASSABLE ROAD THEY ALIGHTED...

...AND FOR MILES SPLASHED ON IN SILENCE THROUGH THE TERRIBLE CYPRESS WOODS...

...WHERE DAY NEVER CAME.

UGLY ROOTS AND MALIGNANT HANGING NOOSES OF SPANISH MOSS BESET THEM...

...AND NOW AND THEN FRAGMENTS OF A ROTTING WALL INTENSIFIED THE MORBID ATMOSPHERE.

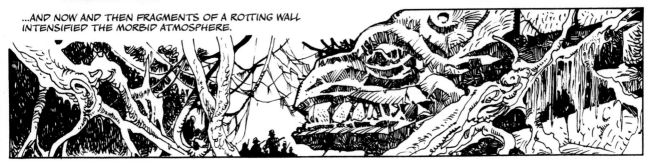

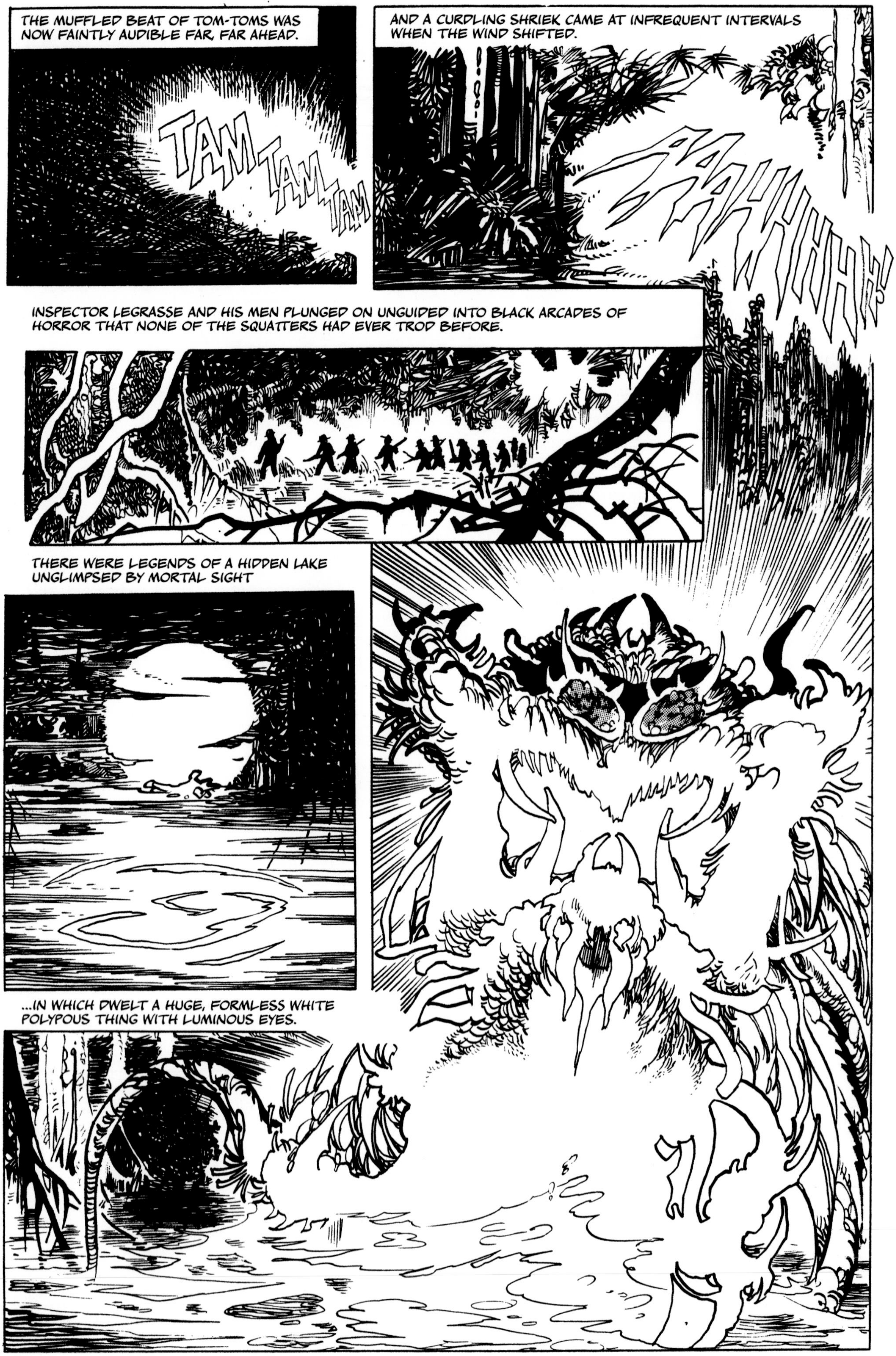
THE MUFFLED BEAT OF TOM-TOMS WAS NOW FAINTLY AUDIBLE FAR, FAR AHEAD.
TAM TAM TAM TAM
AND A CURDLING SHRIEK CAME AT INFREQUENT INTERVALS WHEN THE WIND SHIFTED.
AAAHHHHH!
INSPECTOR LEGRASSE AND HIS MEN PLUNGED ON UNGUIDED INTO BLACK ARCADES OF HORROR THAT NONE OF THE SQUATTERS HAD EVER TROD BEFORE.
THERE WERE LEGENDS OF A HIDDEN LAKE UNGLIMPSED BY MORTAL SIGHT
...IN WHICH DWELT A HUGE, FORMLESS WHITE POLYPOUS THING WITH LUMINOUS EYES.

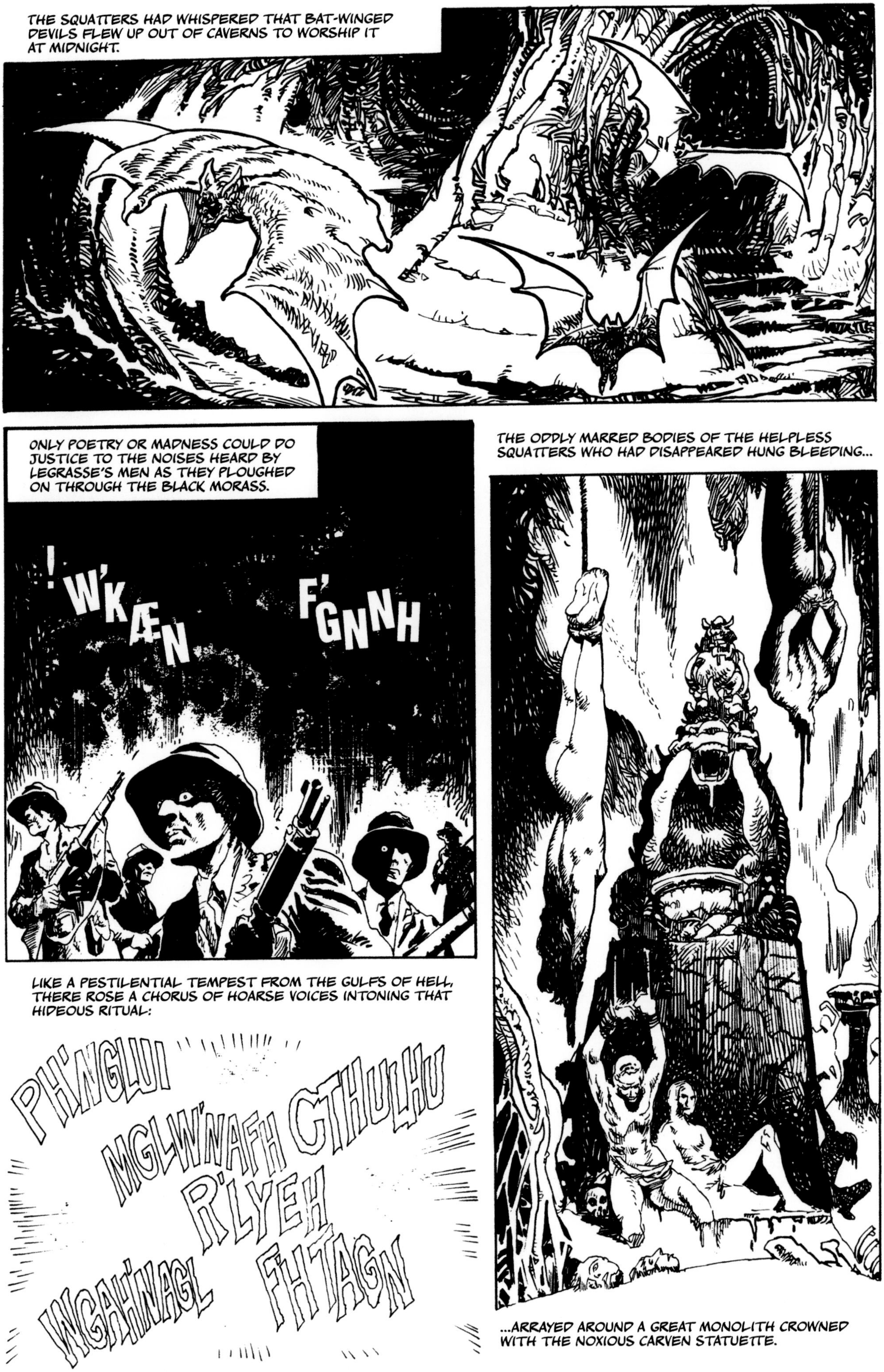
THE SQUATTERS HAD WHISPERED THAT BAT-WINGED DEVILS FLEW UP OUT OF CAVERNS TO WORSHIP IT AT MIDNIGHT.
ONLY POETRY OR MADNESS COULD DO JUSTICE TO THE NOISES HEARD BY LEGRASSE'S MEN AS THEY PLOUGHED ON THROUGH THE BLACK MORASS.
!W'KÆN
F'GNNH
LIKE A PESTILENTIAL TEMPEST FROM THE GULFS OF HELL, THERE ROSE A CHORUS OF HOARSE VOICES INTONING THAT HIDEOUS RITUAL:
PH'NGLUI MGLW'NAFH CTHULHU R'LYEH WGAH'NAGL FHTAGN
THE ODDLY MARRED BODIES OF THE HELPLESS SQUATTERS WHO HAD DISAPPEARED HUNG BLEEDING...
...ARRAYED AROUND A GREAT MONOLITH CROWNED WITH THE NOXIOUS CARVEN STATUETTE.

VOID OF CLOTHING, A HORDE OF HYBRID SPAWN WERE BRAYING, BELLOWING, AND WRITHING TO THE BEAT OF THOSE FRANTIC TOM-TOMS.

THE POLICE RELIED ON THEIR FIREARMS AND PLUNGED DETERMINEDLY INTO THE NAUSEOUS ROUT.

BANG!

BANG!

THE DIN WAS BEYOND DESCRIPTION...

...BUT LEGRASSE WAS ABLE TO TAKE QUITE A FEW PRISONERS.

EXAMINED AT HEADQUARTERS AFTER A TRIP OF INTENSE STRAIN, THEY CONFESSED TO BELONG TO A CULT FAR DEEPER AND OLDER THAN NEGRO FETICHISM.

THEY WORSHIPPED, SO THEY SAID, THE GREAT OLD ONES WHO CAME TO THE YOUNG WORLD OUT OF THE SKY. THEY WERE GONE NOW, INSIDE THE EARTH AND UNDER THE SEA.

BUT THEIR DEAD BODIES HAD TOLD THEIR SECRETS IN DREAMS TO THE FIRST MEN, WHO FORMED A CULT THAT WOULD ALWAYS EXIST, UNTIL THE TIME WHEN THE GREAT PRIEST CTHULHU, FROM HIS DARK HOUSE IN THE MIGHTY CITY OF R'LYEH UNDER THE WATERS, SHOULD RISE...

...AND BRING THE EARTH AGAIN BENEATH HIS SWAY.

CHOSEN MEN HAD TALKED WITH THE ENTOMBED OLD ONES IN DREAMS...

...AND THEN THE GREAT STONE CITY R'LYEH, WITH ITS MONOLITHS AND SEPULCHRES, HAD SUNK BENEATH THE WAVES.

HERE ENDED MY UNCLE'S ACCOUNT OF THESE MATTERS. ONE LAST NOTE EXPLAINED HIS FASCINATION WITH THE YOUNG SCULPTOR AND POLICE INSPECTOR:

THE TWO STATUES WERE *IDENTICAL!*

THE MATTER CAPTIVATED ME SO THAT I MADE SEVERAL JOURNEYS TO PERSONALLY CORROBORATE THE STORIES. BOTH WILCOX AND INSPECTOR LAGRASSE WERE ENTIRELY SINCERE.

ONE THING I BEGAN TO SUSPECT, AND WHICH I NOW FEAR I KNOW, IS THAT MY UNCLE'S DEATH WAS FAR FROM NATURAL. WHETHER I SHALL GO AS HE DID REMAINS TO BE SEEN, FOR I HAVE LEARNED MUCH NOW.

THE MADNESS FROM THE SEA

I HAD LARGELY GIVEN OVER MY INQUIRIES INTO WHAT MY UNCLE CALLED THE "CTHULHU CULT", WHEN BY MERE CHANCE I STUMBLED ON A CLUE THAT WOULD UNRAVEL THAT WHOLE MESS.

IT WAS AN OLD NUMBER OF AN AUSTRALIAN JOURNAL, THE SYDNEY BULLETIN FOR APRIL 18, 1925.

INSIDE WAS A HALF-TONE CUT OF A HIDEOUS STONE IMAGE ALMOST IDENTICAL WITH THAT WHICH LEGRASSE HAD FOUND IN THE SWAMP.

THE HEADLINE READ: "MYSTERY DERELICT FOUND AT SEA"

THE SOLE SURVIVOR HAD BEEN FOUND CLUTCHING THE STATUETTE. HE WAS A NORWEGIAN SAILOR, GUSTAF JOHANSEN.

I RESOLVED TO VISIT JOHANSEN AND, LESS THAN A MONTH LATER, SAILED FOR OSLO TO CONTINUE MY INVESTIGATION.

I MADE MY WAY TO HIS HOUSE, WHERE TERRIBLE NEWS AWAITED ME: GUSTAF JOHANSEN WAS NO MORE. HIS WIFE KNEW NOTHING OF HIS FATEFUL VOYAGE.

PHYSICIANS HAD FOUND NO ADEQUATE CAUSE FOR THE SAILOR'S DEATH.

I NOW FELT GNAWING AT MY VITALS THAT DARK TERROR WHICH WILL NEVER LEAVE ME TILL I, TOO, AM AT REST; "ACCIDENTALLY" OR OTHERWISE.

THE WIDOW GAVE ME A MANUSCRIPT IN ENGLISH THAT HAD BELONGED TO HER HUSBAND, AND I BEGAN TO READ IT ON THE BOAT TO LONDON.

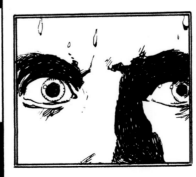

IN THIS POST-FACTO DIARY, JOHANSEN HAD ATTEMPTED TO RECALL DAY BY DAY THAT LAST AWFUL VOYAGE.

GUSTAF JOHANSEN HAD BEEN THE SECOND MATE OF THE TWO-MASTED SCHOONER EMMA.

THE CREW CONSISTED OF ELEVEN MEN, EXPERT SAILORS. BUT THE SHIP WAS THROWN WIDELY OFF HER COURSE BY A GREAT STORM ON MARCH 1ST.

AFTER SOME DAYS OF SAILING, THE EMMA WAS HELD UP BY A VESSEL...

...MANNED BY A QUEER AND EVIL-LOOKING CREW OF KANAKAS AND HALF-CASTES WHO ORDERED THEM TO TURN BACK.

THE STRANGE SHIP THEN BEGAN TO FIRE SAVAGELY AND WITHOUT WARNING...

BOOOM!!

THOUGH THE SCHOONER BEGAN TO SINK, THE EMMA MANAGED TO HEAVE ALONGSIDE THEIR ENEMY AND BOARD HER...

...GRAPPLING WITH THE SAVAGE CREW ON THE YACHT'S DECK.

THE PIRATES' MODE OF FIGHTING WAS ABHORRENT AND DESPERATE THOUGH RATHER CLUMSY...

CRACK BANG BANG BANG

...AND THE BATTLE DID NOT END UNTIL THEY'D BEEN FORCED TO KILL THEM ALL.

THREE OF THE EMMA'S MEN DIED, INCLUDING THE CAPTAIN.

THE REMAINING EIGHT UNDER SECOND MATE
JOHANSEN PROCEEDED TO NAVIGATE, TRYING
TO SEE IF ANY REASON FOR THEIR ORDERING
BACK HAD EXISTED.

AT S. LATITUDE 47° 9', W. LONGITUDE
126° 43', THEY SPOTTED A SMALL ISLAND
THAT DID NOT APPEAR ON THEIR MAPS.

THE MEN SIGHTED A GREAT STONE
PILLAR STICKING OUT OF THE SEA...

...AN OOZING CYCLOPEAN MONOLITH WHICH SEEMED THE TANGIBLE SUBSTANCE
OF EARTH'S SUPREME TERROR.

IT COULD BE NONE OTHER THAN THE NIGHTMARE CORPSE-CITY OF **R'LYEH,** BUILT IN MEASURELESS AEONS BEHIND HISTORY BY THE VAST, LOATHSOME SHAPES THAT SEEPED DOWN FROM THE DARK STARS. THERE LAY GREAT CTHULHU AND HIS HORDES, HIDDEN IN GREEN SLIMY VAULTS.

JOHANSEN AND HIS MEN LANDED AT A SLOPING MUD-BANK ON THIS MONSTROUS ACROPOLIS.

SOMETHING VERY LIKE FRIGHT CAME OVER ALL THE EXPLORERS, FOR THIS COULD HAVE BEEN NO MORTAL STAIRCASE.

THEY CLAMBERED SLIPPERILY UP OVER TITAN OOZY BLOCKS.

IT WAS RODRIGUEZ THE PORTUGUESE WHO SHOUTED OF WHAT HE HAD FOUND.

THE REST FOLLOWED HIM AND LOOKED CURIOUSLY AT THE IMMENSE CARVED DOOR.

AT THAT MOMENT, THE ACRE-GREAT PANEL BEGAN TO GIVE INWARD.

THE ODOR ARISING FROM THE NEWLY OPENED DEPTHS WAS INTOLERABLE.

THEY HEARD AN OTHERWORLDLY SLOPPING SOUND COMING FROM THE ALMOST MATERIAL DARKNESS.

SPTUUUG...

IT LUMBERED SLOBBERINGLY INTO SIGHT AND GROPINGLY SQUEEZED ITS GELATINOUS GREEN IMMENSITY THROUGH THE BLACK DOORWAY INTO THE TAINTED OUTSIDE AIR OF THAT POISON CITY OF MADNESS.

JOHANSEN THINKS TWO MEN PERISHED OF PURE FRIGHT IN THAT ACCURSED INSTANT.

THE THING OF THE IDOLS, THE GREEN, STICKY SPAWN OF THE STARS, HAD AWAKED TO CLAIM HIS OWN.

OF THE OTHER MEN WHO NEVER REACHED THE SHIP, JOHANSEN THINKS THEY WERE SWALLOWED UP INTO THE BEING.

ONLY BRIDEN AND JOHANSEN
REACHED THE ROW BOAT...

...AND DESPERATELY TRIED TO ESCAPE.

THE PIRATE SHIP'S STEAM ENGINES HAD GONE OUT AND IT TOOK A FEW MOMENTS TO GET THE SHIP MOVING.

.. POF POF POF ..

IN THE MEANTIME, THE MOUNTAINOUS MONSTROSITY FLOPPED DOWN THE SLIMY STONES...

...AND HESITATED FLOUNDERING AT THE EDGE OF THE SEA.

AT LAST THE THING FROM THE STARS SLID GIBBERING INTO THE WATER...

...BRIDEN LOOKED BACK AND WAS RENDERED MAD TILL DEATH TOOK PITY ON HIM.

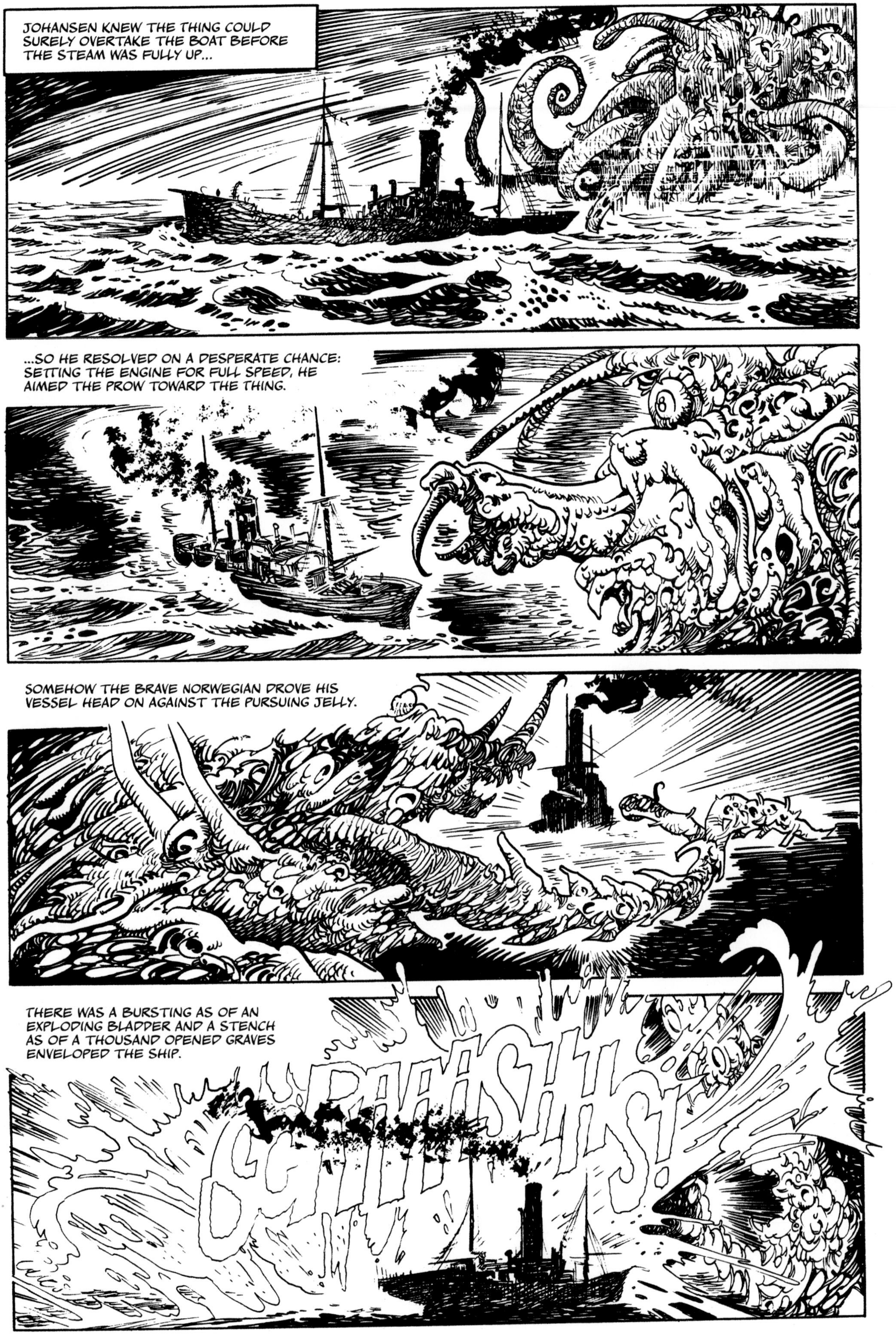
JOHANSEN KNEW THE THING COULD SURELY OVERTAKE THE BOAT BEFORE THE STEAM WAS FULLY UP...
...SO HE RESOLVED ON A DESPERATE CHANCE: SETTING THE ENGINE FOR FULL SPEED, HE AIMED THE PROW TOWARD THE THING.
SOMEHOW THE BRAVE NORWEGIAN DROVE HIS VESSEL HEAD ON AGAINST THE PURSUING JELLY.
THERE WAS A BURSTING AS OF AN EXPLODING BLADDER AND A STENCH AS OF A THOUSAND OPENED GRAVES ENVELOPED THE SHIP.

FOR AN INSTANT THE SHIP WAS BEFOULED BY AN ACRID AND BLINDING GREEN CLOUD, AND THEN THERE WAS ONLY A VENOMOUS SEETHING ASTERN.

SQUINTING THROUGH THE MUDDY AIR, JOHANSEN SAW WITH HORROR HOW THAT NAMELESS SKY-SPAWN WAS NEBULOUSLY RECOMBINING, WHILST ITS DISTANCE WIDENED EVERY SECOND AS THE SHIP GAINED IMPETUS FROM ITS MOUNTING STEAM.

THAT WAS ALL. HE DID NOT TRY TO NAVIGATE. HE FELT SOMETHING HAD BEEN TAKEN OUT OF HIS SOUL.

OF COURSE HE COULD NOT TELL WHAT HE HAD SEEN. EVERYONE WOULD THINK HIM MAD.

AFTER THAT CAME THE RESCUE. HE WOULD WRITE OF WHAT HE KNEW BEFORE DEATH CAME. DEATH WOULD BE A BOON IF ONLY IT COULD BLOT OUT THE MEMORIES.

THAT WAS THE LAST DOCUMENT I READ, AND NOW I HAVE PLACED IT IN MY UNCLE'S TIN BOX.

I DO NOT THINK MY LIFE WILL BE LONG. I KNOW TOO MUCH.

CTHULHU LIVES!

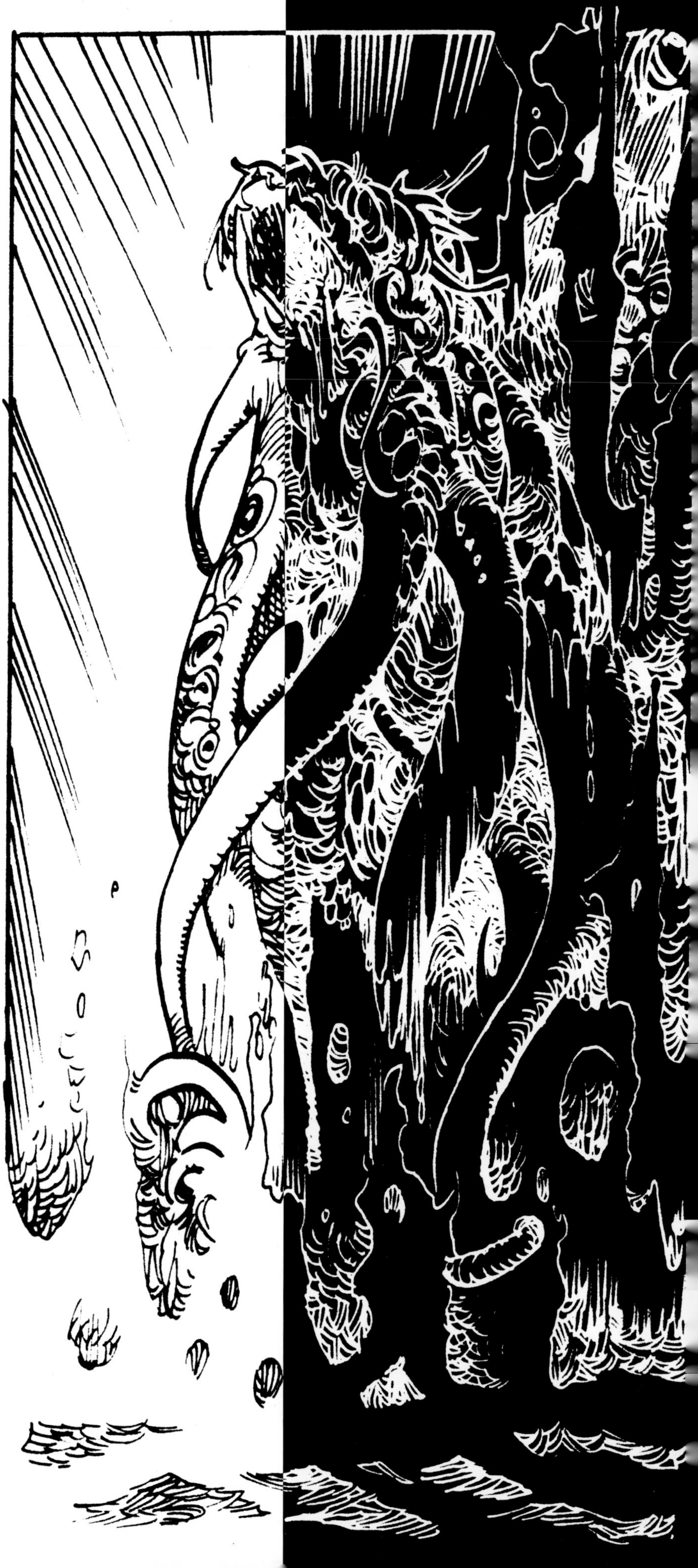

Esteban Maroto

LOVECRAFT
THE MYTH OF CTHULHU

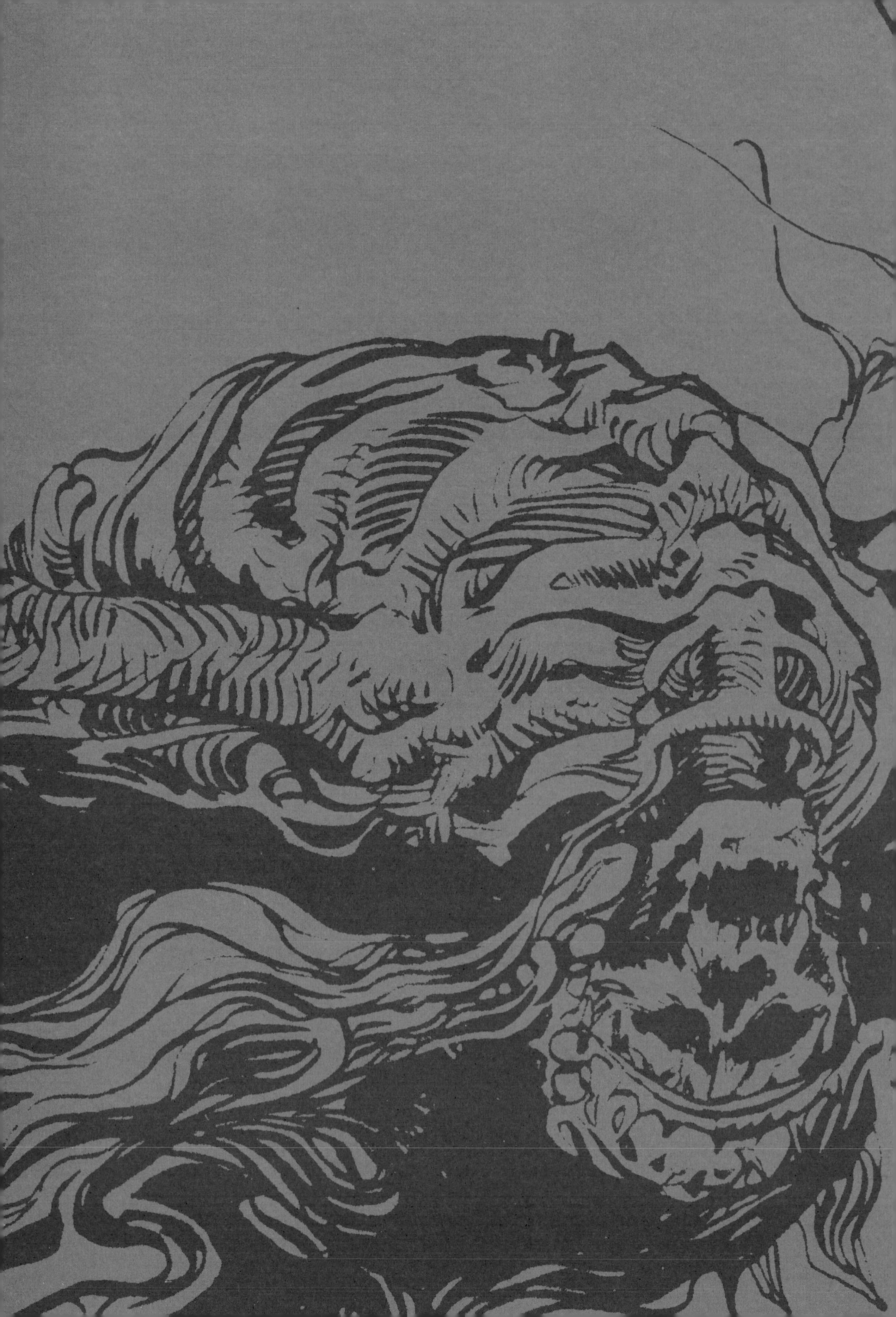